"From laughter to tears, Paul weaves God's truth throughout this starkly honest collection of letters. A must read for anyone looking into making the 'second most important decision in life.' In a loving way, Paul shows my wife Emily and me how to set the bar high for our daughters. Wisdom beyond years is contained in this timeless book."

Grant Williams
Former offensive linesman for the Saint Louis Rams, St. Louis, MO

"Paul Friesen is a man's man whom God blessed with a family of women. After a lifetime of ministry to other people's families, through letters to his three daughters, Paul gives us glimpses of conversations that have shaped their relationship choices and guided their spiritual development. His wisdom, integrity, humor, and love are revealed in these 52 snapshots of life with a godly father. The reader will learn what it is to live each day with the 'end game' in mind, that of becoming independent, competent, contented young women who love and serve the Lord Jesus Christ with a joyful heart."

Howard Clark
Senior Pastor, First Evangelical Church, Memphis, TN

"What a gift! As a father of two very young daughters, I praise God for Paul Friesen and his book *Letters to My Daughters*. Throughout these imaginative letters, Paul's love for his family and biblical truth are clearly evident. With every turn of the page, you will be challenged to raise children who accept nothing short of God's best. As my daughters grow, I plan to reference this book early and often and I hope you will do the same."

Danny Oertli
Author and Songwriter, Parker, CO

"These letters have meant so much to me, as my husband, Paul, can tell you by the number of times he's had to recopy them for me. I will cherish the book as a unique tool to navigate the waters of parenting a coming-of-age daughter or son. I so appreciate Paul Friesen's wisdom, especially about the female's responsibility to be careful about the type of lures she uses and where she fishes."

Kate Wylie
Wife of Paul Wylie, Olympic champion ice skater, Charlotte, NC

"I love how each letter addresses the lies that are so prevalent in our culture in regards to sex and dating. They were an amazing resource to me as I pursued my wife-to-be with the desire to have a Christ-centered relationship. Though written to girls, it gave me a clear picture of who I needed to be as a man in the relationship so that I was a worthy suitor who would fulfill my God-given responsibilities as a leader who could love the way Christ called me to love."

Brian Dietz
Junior High Youth Pastor, Grace Chapel, Lexington, MA

"I have actually used them in family devotionals, around the dinner table, and as forwarded advice to friends. Many of them speak to issues that parents want children to know and think about, but need to be reinforced by yet another voice. Even though they are written to older daughters, my younger crew (ages 8–13) benefit by bringing up moral issues that stimulate discussion for teaching and reinforcement that should and can begin at any age. These letters are inspiring tools to guide children and influence parents both at the same time. The personalized letters from a father to his daughters are written with compassion and a heartfelt voice."

Melanie Bilazarian
Massachusetts

"Although these letters came into my life after my children were grown, they have helped me to communicate more effectively with all of my children as adults. They give me the tools that I need to articulate my thoughts in a non-threatening way. I now have the opportunity to help my grandchildren set a vision for their lives that they will be able to embrace. Your letters have truly been an inspiration to me. Thank you for sharing your letters with all of us."

Charlotte Dean
Massachusetts

"I had a chance to read one of your letters while the twins are sleeping. You are an outstanding dad. I will rely on your letters to help Kevin and me give this advice to our three girls someday. I am already praying that they will follow the Lord and walk in the truth. I also pray for their sexual purity. I am so thankful that you have shared these letters with us. What a blessing! Also, when the time is right and my girls get older, I will let them read the letters. Thank you very much for the outstanding advice!"

Kim Gannon
New Hampshire

Letters to My Daughters

A dad's thoughts on a most important decision—

Marriage

Paul A. Friesen

Home Improvement Ministries
Bedford, Massachusetts

LETTERS TO MY DAUGHTERS:
A Dad's Thoughts on a Most Important Decision—Marriage
Paul A. Friesen

Copyright © 2006 by Paul A. Friesen
Cover illustration and cover design: Michael Benes
Interior design and production: Barbara Steele
Copyediting: Guy Steele

ISBN-13: 978-0-9789931-0-8
ISBN-10: 0-9789931-0-1

Home Improvement Ministries
209 Burlington Road
Bedford, MA 01730

Find us on the web at: www.HIMweb.org

Unless otherwise noted, all scripture quotations are from the HOLY BIBLE:
NEW INTERNATIONAL VERSION. Copyright © 1973, 1978, 1984 by the
International Bible Society.

Other versions used are:

HCSB	Scripture quotations marked HCSB are been taken from the Holman Christian Standard Bible®, Copyright © 1999, 2000, 2002, 2003 by Holman Bible Publishers. Used by permission. Holman Christian Standard Bible®, Holman CSB®, and HCSB® are federally registered trademarks of Holman Bible Publishers.
MSG	Scripture taken from The Message. Copyright © 1993, 1994, 1995, 1996, 2000, 2001, 2002. Used by permission of NavPress Publishing Group.
NASB	Scripture taken from the NEW AMERICAN STANDARD BIBLE®, Copyright © 1960, 1962, 1963, 1968, 1971, 1972, 1973, 1975, 1977, 1995 by The Lockman Foundation. Used by permission.

Second printing, November 2006
Printed in the United States of America.   11/18-06TPS4000

To Dr. Virginia "Bun" Friesen

Asking you to marry me was the second best decision of my life.
Thanks for saying "yes."
You are the best wife and mother to our girls
I could ever imagine.

I love you more today than yesterday—
but not as much as tomorrow.

Contents

Foreword

As a pastor, I see thousands of parents pack Bayside Church each weekend, many with a deep desire for their kids not only to grow up with character and convictions, but eventually to marry men and women of strong character and convictions as well. Most of these parents feel ill-equipped for the task of helping that happen.

I can relate! As a parent of four teenagers (Mark, 18; Scott, 16; and 14-year-old twin daughters, Christy and Leslie), I need all the ideas I can get! However, I prefer getting ideas that actually work from authentic people that I actually trust. In this book, Paul Friesen has provided both the encouragement and equipping to meet that need.

Letters To My Daughters was born out a lifetime of parenting and pastoring, and I am excited about recommending it to you for two reasons:

First, I know Paul Friesen well. Very well! He and his wife Virginia have influenced my life and parenting as much as anyone on the planet. Speaking together, working together, and vacationing together gave us the opportunity to develop a deep friendship. We have prayed for each other's kids, cheered each other on during the successes, and had some late night phone calls during the tough times. I have benefited greatly from hundreds of in-depth conversations about developing godly character, handling first dates and first rebellions, and helping our kids become G-rated people in an X-rated world. I have grown as a husband and parent and have no doubt that as you spend the next few hours with Paul and his daughters in this book, his insights on relationships will have the same impact on you.

Second, I know his daughters well. Very well! One of his daughters, Kari, is on our staff full-time working with teenagers—and I am ready to hire Lisa and Julie any time they are ready! They have had all the ups and downs of all of our kids, but bottom line, they are making wise choices about relationships. Why? Because of their commitment to Christ and because of the wisdom shared with them over the years by their parents—and most recently, specifically by their dad in this collection of letters.

I know you (and your children) will benefit as well. Whether you are reading for yourself or reading for ideas to pass on to your kids, know that what you are about to read in this book works!

Ray Johnston, Senior Pastor
Bayside Covenant Church
Granite Bay, California

About These Letters

Having three daughters has been one of the greatest joys of my life. My wife Virginia and I have enjoyed and been challenged by each stage of our girls' lives. I must say, however, that this latest stage of their lives has brought more joy than any other. I love being able to hang out with them, adult-to-adult. I love being referred to as "Kari's dad," "Lisa's dad," and "Julie's dad." At the same time as this unparalleled joy, they are now making most of their own decisions without "ol' Dad" being there. And one of the most significant decisions before them is the decision regarding marriage.

About three years ago I started to email Kari, Lisa, and Julie a series of letters sharing some thoughts regarding the second most important decision of their lives: marriage. As their friends at college started to hear about these letters, they asked to be added to the email list of those receiving them. And as parents in our classes at church started to hear about the letters, they asked for copies as well.

To make a long story short, in the end we were eventually encouraged to compile these letters into a book. Although the original letters were written in random order as topics came to mind, they have been sorted here into four major categories. Each section discusses certain characteristics of a potential spouse (and also of the reader) that should be considered before marriage. Some characteristics are matters of preference and compatibility; others should be regarded as non-negotiable.

The initial few letters are introductory in nature. Following those are letters in the *Convictions* section, which address spiritual matters. Here, a mismatch with one's potential spouse should be a "deal stopper." These include having a personal relationship with Christ, the source of ultimate authority in one's life, and commitment to God's Word.

The section on *Character* introduces traits that are critical to a vibrant marriage: Does your potential spouse have a "servant heart"? (And do you?) Is he a person of integrity? Is he willing to truly leave his mother and father and cleave to his wife?

Letters in *Considerations* cover issues of compatibility. A few differences in these areas may not merit breaking an engagement, but if enough differences are counted up, there may be reason to pause and think, to discuss, or to seek counsel. Living with a mate who enjoys what you enjoy is much more enjoyable!

The *Chemistry* section includes letters that address the need for (and the implications of) physical and emotional attraction and how to handle them before marriage. While chemistry is vital to a thriving marriage, if experienced too deeply too soon, it can cloud one's vision and judgment.

The final letters offer summary insights from a dad who longs for each of his precious daughters—as well as every reader of these letters—to be better equipped to find, recognize, and appreciate the spouse she (or he) has always wanted.

These letters were written specifically with Kari, Lisa, and Julie in mind. I realize each relationship is unique, but my prayer is that the issues raised may also be helpful and clarifying to you and may help you to make wise decisions as you face the "second most important decision" in your life.

Some Memories...
Some Dreams

Dear Kari, Lisa, and Julie,

What a year it has been. I turned fifty, Kari turned 21, Lisa 18, Julie 16—and your mom continues to be a fountain of youth and vitality. I consider these to be the best days of life: a home with four women who all love the Lord, usually love each other, and are kind to dear old Dad.

What could be better? I have loved every stage of your life, but the teen years have been especially wonderful. Naturally, they have not come without challenges! Remember the time Kari snuck out and went to a movie with a boy while your mom and I were away? Worse, she then lied to us about it when Julie inadvertently spilled the beans. (Julie saw your mom crying one day and said, "Are you crying about Kari sneaking out and going to the movie with Tim?").

I also remember the time Lisa was caught on the soccer field of her Christian high school by a teacher while trying to see what kissing a guy really felt like. Or the time your youth leader came to me after a service and told me he was praying for our family during this "tough time." I asked Julie on the way home from church what it was the youth leaders were praying about. She said she had just shared the tension she was having with her sisters and had asked the youth group to pray.

Some of my favorite memories are of family camp, when all three of you would come in at the 11:00 PM curfew each night, sit on our bed, and tell us of your day's activities. At home, I love it when you come in early in the morning (or late at night) and climb onto the bed with us just to talk a bit before the day begins (or ends).

> Whether or not you marry—and if you do, whom you marry—will influence virtually every other decision you ever make.

Remember the "Daddy/daughter" dinners we used to have when just the four of us would go out to Friendly's and have three kid's meals and an adult entree? Remember our 90-day cross-country camping trip, and our trip to Germany to visit Kari while she was in Bible School? Remember our family nights every Tuesday, and my Saturday waffles?

Although reminiscing is fun, the real purpose of the letters to follow is to put on paper some thoughts regarding the second most important decision of life: marriage. I am thankful that each of you has made the *most* important decision: to follow Christ. I claim that marriage is the second most important decision because whether or not you marry—and if you do, whom you marry—will influence virtually every other decision you ever make.

As you know, your mom and I have enjoyed 25 years of marriage. It has not all been perfect, but on the whole it has been a wonderful relationship of partnership and love. You yourselves know—not even counting all our stories from counseling couples—how the lives of your own cousins, aunts, and uncles have been so clearly affected by their choices in mates.

As I start these letters, let me say clearly that God's best gift to you may be singleness. It is much better to be single in God's will, than married outside of His best.

I love you each dearly. I am so thankful God saw fit to give me such a great wife and mother to our children, as well as you three delightful girls. It goes without saying that even though I am writing these letters, they reflect the thoughts of both your mom and me. We are one, you know.

Love, Dad

The Second Most Important Decision

Dear Kari, Lisa, and Julie,

I know this first observation is not new to you—in fact, I imagine there will not be much in these letters that is new, but it will make your Dad feel a bit better to put this thought in writing: who you choose as a mate is the second most important decision you will ever make. As you know, the most important decision has to do with your relationship with Jesus Christ.

Your mom and I spend hours each week counseling couples who are in marital crisis. Many of them are there because they made very unwise decisions regarding whom to marry. As we have often said before, the most important decision in life is whether or not to follow the Lord, and the second most important decision in life is whom to marry.

I think of two sisters in our church. Both had the same parents, were raised in the same home, and had the same opportunities. Today, one is married to an educated, responsible man who provides for and leads his family in a God-pleasing way. The other is in a very difficult marriage, with significant problems in her life and in the lives of her children. The main difference in these two women's lives is *who* they married.

As you know, I perform many weddings each year. When

a couple arrives in my office to plan the ceremony with me, I don't start out by asking how long they plan to be married. ("If you are planning on staying married for twenty years or more, the wedding is quite involved. However, if you anticipate being married for two years or less, I am able to perform a very short ceremony that is not complex at all!") Most couples who walk down the aisle *plan* to be married a lifetime—yet few will accomplish this.

Because I love you so much and wish the best for you, I am going to attempt to put on paper some tips, ideas, principles, and truths from God's Word regarding preparation for marriage—or more specifically, on how to choose a great mate. I certainly don't think I have it all together, nor do I have all the answers, but I will tell you one thing: your mom and I haven't poured our lives into yours for all these years only to watch you marry someone who will not cherish you, serve you, love you, and care for you as Christ cared for the church. Yes, I agree, it's hard for me to imagine that I will feel anyone is "good enough" for my girls, but I do want you to have every advantage possible as you consider whom you will spend the rest of your life with, and who will be the father of your children.

I know of your deep commitment to Christ. But I also am aware that you are human and that each of us deeply desires to have an intimate relationship with another. I want for each of you to find that intimacy first in Christ, and then in one who loves Christ supremely and will honor you as His (and my) precious daughter.

I love you the whole wide world—
Dad

Jetta Trip—
Not Like It Used to Be

Dear Kari, Lisa, and Julie,

On my road trip across the country a few years ago to bring
the Jetta to Lisa, I came across only one accident in three days
of driving. The accident, however, shut the highway down for
a half-hour. Apparently, the driver was going pretty fast across
the high desert when he fell asleep, ran off the road, and did a
series of flips, completely mangling the car. The LifeFlight heli-
copter took the driver up and away. Whether he survived or not,
I'll never know.

Driving across those flat desert roads reminded me of a story
about your great-grandfather and great-grandmother on my
mother's side. They were traveling cross-country, driving late into
the night on a flat stretch very similar to the road I was on. As
the story goes, your great-grandmother suddenly shouted to her
husband, "Latimer! Latimer! What is that string of lights over
there?" Awakened by her shouting, he calmly said, "Why, Laura,
I suppose those would be the cars on the highway." Latimer had
fallen asleep, but because the speed of the car was so slow and
the ride so rough anyway, neither of them realized he had driven
off the road over the open desert. Well! They headed over to the
string of lights and soon were back on the road again.

The reason I am sharing this story is that both drivers apparently did the same thing—but one was a bit embarrassed and the other likely dead. You see, going off the road in 1930 was significantly different from going off the road in 2003.

As I was driving the Jetta for those several days, I had plenty of time to think. One of the things I reflected upon was a comment a mom made to me after hearing your mother and me speak at a True Love Waits seminar. We had talked about what we felt were scriptural guidelines for physical involvement in dating. We suggested that anything from French kissing on would be considered foreplay and inappropriate for anyone before marriage.

After the session the mom came up to me and said, "My high school son and his girlfriend are out together virtually every night. I never have talked to him about physical boundaries—I just assumed they were making out. After all," she said, "my husband and I made out all the time when we were dating."

> Living according to God's word in the area of relationships is critical.

I told her that making out then and making out now are about as different as driving off the road at 30 mph and driving off the road at 90 mph. I am not saying that what she and her husband were doing was right back then; however, there are definitely some differences. For instance, 30 years ago, sleeping with someone before you got married was still seen as "wrong" by our culture. It is what the "bad" girls did. (I still don't totally understand why it was only the *girls* who were considered bad.) There were still cultural values that encouraged certain restraints between couples before marriage. For those who did become sexually active, there were five sexually transmitted diseases known at the time, all of them treatable. Today there are over thirty sexually transmitted diseases—and over half of these are incurable, lifelong diseases, some of which are fatal.

I am telling you these stories to underscore why living according to God's word in the area of relationships is so critical. It was wrong to go off the road back then, but few ever died as a result. Today the risks of driving are much greater. So it is in the area of relationships. It has always been best to follow God's word in this area, but now the risks of disobedience are even greater.

Your mom and I are so thankful for the decisions you have made to follow the Lord in the area of relationships. You will hear many people say that "off roading" will not hurt you. Few will tell you that the best way to drive is *at* the speed limit, and *on* the highway. I am thankful that your mom and I had parents that taught us the pleasures of driving responsibly and the dangers of driving irresponsibly. I am also thankful that they taught us the importance of living responsibly with our sexuality. We do not want to be negligent by not sharing God's "driving instructions" with you.

It just struck me that there are different speed limits posted, depending on the road conditions and areas of travel, such as residential areas, etc. At one o'clock this morning, a policeman turned on his flashing blue lights to help a disabled car. A 15- and a 16-year-old were out driving alone—which is against the law because of the hour and because of the age of the passenger. The boys saw the patroller's lights, and assuming the lights were meant for them, took off speeding through town to avoid being stopped. They lost control of the car and it hit a tree, killing both boys. They violated the laws that had been set up for their safety and died because of it. They missed out on years of driving on the open road where high speeds were permitted, because they tried to go at high speeds in places not appropriate. Not only will they never experience driving at high speeds; they will never experience life.

I'm sure you see the analogy. God has designed us to thrill at high-speed rides down the highway, but He warns us not to go at such speeds until on roads approved for such activity. Sexual involvement in marriage is wonderful, but many have missed out on the thrill of sexual expression in marriage because they have gone too far, too fast, too soon.

Enjoy the journey!

Love, Dad

Convictions

Introduction

Character

Considerations

Chemistry

Concluding Thoughts

Epilogue

A Man Whole
Without You

Dear Kari, Lisa, and Julie,

As you've heard me say before, who you choose as a mate is the second most important decision you will ever make, and the most important decision has to do with your relationship with Jesus Christ.

It might seem obvious, but is often missed, that the most important characteristic in a mate is *his or her* relationship with Christ. I will refer to this truth many times as I write. However, right now I want to focus on one aspect of *why* this is so important.

The word that most often describes marriage in scripture is "oneness." In Matthew 19[1] we are told that "the two will become one." Note that it does not mean two *halves* become one, but that two *wholes* become one. This clearly implies that before we marry we need to be relatively whole ourselves. Sometimes our well-meaning married friends talk about their "better half." It is easy for us to believe then that we are "worse halves" in search of a "better half" so that we might become complete.

Colossians 2:10[2] makes it very clear that our completeness comes from Christ and not from another person. In his book *The Marriage Builder*, Larry Crabb[3] states that if our wholeness, significance, and worth are found in our mates, we have given them too much power over us. What he is saying is that if my real happiness, fulfillment, and meaning in life are found only in another person, I have given her the power to destroy me. But if my significance, worth, and completeness come from Christ, my mate can hurt me deeply, but she can't destroy me.

Your mother and I know a woman whose husband divorced her after many years of marriage. The divorce was devastating and hurt this woman a great deal. But it did not destroy her, because she had a vital relationship with Christ and knew *He* was the source of her significance.

How does this apply *before* marriage—or, how can you see this in another person? I'll tell you how I saw it in your mom: one of the things that first attracted me to your mom (besides her legs) was the fact that she didn't seem to need me. She was very involved in life and seemed quite content as a single person. I, too, was busy with ministry and was

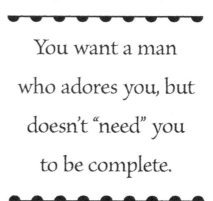

You want a man who adores you, but doesn't "need" you to be complete.

not "seeking" someone to make my life complete. Later, when your mom and I were dating, we would see greeting cards with endearments such as, "The grass was always brown until I met you" (they were describing the grass one *mows*), or "The sky was always gray until I met you," and so on. Those thoughts simply did not apply to our case. We were delightfully happy before we met each other. In one sense, what attracted us to one other was the fact that we didn't "need" each other.

Now, don't get me wrong. We had a blast together and much preferred being together rather than apart. As I write this letter, your mom is away for a few days and I feel like a part of me is missing. This is theologically correct, since "the two have become one, they are no longer two." Something mysterious happens when you become one with another person. It isn't that you can't function without each other, but there is a sense that when you are apart, all is not as it was designed to be. As Jesus says, referring to divorce in Matthew 19, Moses may have allowed it, but "it was not this way from the beginning."[4]

Therefore, you want a man who adores you, but doesn't "need" you to be complete. Perhaps a good way to visualize this is to think of two glasses of water, one full and the other one almost empty. In order to make them equal, the full glass will need to fill the other glass—and afterwards it won't be as full as it would have been if the other glass had started out full as well. But two glasses that start out full can remain full when put together.

I have a friend who was a very strong Christian and had planned to go into ministry. He married a woman who was not a strong Christian. As a result, he had to put his goal to be a pastor on hold for many years while he focused on helping his wife's "glass" become more full.

Each of you are strong Christians—for which your mom and I are extremely thankful. I wish for each of you a man who will be independently strong in His relationship with Christ.

+ Is he is a man of prayer?
+ Does he love God's word?
+ Is he involved in a local church?
+ Does his lifestyle reflect that of Christ?
+ Does he share your passion for ministry?
+ Does he lead in spiritual or moral issues, or do you find yourself initiating and leading more?

At a later date I'll write about physical involvement in marriage, but let me illustrate for you how you can tell a great deal about a man by how he acts toward you in this area: is *he* the one who takes the initiative in setting the boundaries for physical involvement, or is this "up to you?" The way he responds to you in the physical area will also tell you a great deal about his willingness to put the interests of another above his own desires. It will tell you something about whether he is a man of self-control.

As you know, your mom and I spend a great deal of time counseling couples in troubled marriages. Your mom counsels countless women individually, as well. We find a common thread in so many of these troubled marriages: one mate is a Christian and the other is not, or one is serious about his or her faith and the other is not.

Well, that's enough for tonight. I love you each more than you will ever know. I long for you to enjoy all God's richest blessings in marriage—and that comes from two people being madly in love with Jesus before they are madly in love with each other.

Love, Dad

Do You Share
a Love for God?

Dear Kari, Lisa, and Julie,

As the last of our camp staff reunion gang left the house this morning, I was again struck with how thankful I am for the choices of friends you have made. In addition to our crazy one-day trip to New York to see *Les Miserables*, sledding at midnight, games of Cranium, and meals with endless conversation and laughter, I especially enjoyed the serendipitous times of deeper conversation.

Though your camp staff friends have many different talents, skills, interests, and passions, they all share a common love for Jesus. Each one of them has made a commitment to abide and grow in Christ. At camp, they work alongside one another to share God's love with others.

So, how important in a relationship is this common interest in Jesus? Today I want to start the first of what will most likely be several letters on the subject of being "unequally yoked."

I don't know much about oxen; however, the word does not seem that flattering to me. I do remember times I have been compared to an ox, as in "You are as clumsy as an ox." In 2 Corinthians 6:14, the apostle Paul says that we are not to be "unequally yoked together with unbelievers."[1] The word picture here is of two oxen pulling a plow or cart. The oxen are "hooked" together with a yoke: basically, a large piece of wood with two slots for the oxen's heads. The image of being unequally yoked is that if you team a large ox with a small ox, the yoke won't fit especially well. So don't marry anyone large, since you are all slender—no, I don't think that is the thrust of Paul's teaching! What Paul is saying is that it works much better when you are teamed with someone like yourself. In the case of oxen, it would be with another ox of similar size, strength, and experience.

In the Corinthians passage, Paul is specifically speaking about marrying unbelievers. He is illustrating the concept that when the most important things in two people's lives are contradictory or opposite one another, then those two people are unequally yoked. They actually will pull against, not with, each other. Scripture is quite clear that there are only two classifications of people: children of God and children of the devil. In the passage on being unequally yoked, Paul goes on to say, "for what do darkness and light have in common?" The point Paul is making is that a Christian and a non-Christian are not to marry each other.

I really like what the late Paul Little once said: "Are you, as a Christian, praying about whether you should marry a non-Christian? Save your breath!"[2] God has clearly stated in scripture that it is not His will for Christians and non-Christians to enter into marriage with one other. Some will argue that this passage speaks only of marriage, not dating. But scripture doesn't address dating at all as we practice it today. So while there may not be specific commands that forbid us to date non-believers, scripture as well as experience give us plenty of reasons to seriously consider whether dating a non-believer is truly the wisest action.

Any time mom and I speak on this subject, someone in the group will say, "My mom married my dad when he wasn't a Christian, and now he is one." I always respond that this is an example of God's grace in the parents' lives, but that for the believing spouse it was still a sinful choice. I also point out that there are many teens who are not present at the meeting because their parents married unequally; the Christian parent no longer is following the Lord, and now, in turn, neither are those teens.

Here is why I think it is best not to date non-Christians: We all long for intimacy with another person. Once we get involved with someone and "fall in love," our thinking often becomes a bit foggy. I remember a friend who "fell in love" with someone who did not appear to be a Christian. When I asked my friend about it, he said, "I think our definition of 'Christian' is often too narrow." He got hooked in the relationship and then started "reinterpreting" scripture so he could justify his relationship. Even King Solomon's heart was turned away from God because he loved his wives who worshipped idols rather than the one true God.[3]

The bottom line is: marry a Christian. But secondly, marry only someone who is "equally yoked" with you in his passion for the Lord.

The bottom line is: marry only a Christian. But secondly, marry only someone who is "equally yoked" with you in his passion for the Lord. We see many spouses who are frustrated because they married a "Christian," but not one who was passionate about following Him.

I long for you to be married to an "ox" who will be a true partner. I don't want you to be dragging that ol' ox around because you have married someone who does not share your love for the Lord. It is better to pull a plow alone than to pull the plow and a slow ox as well.

I love you the whole wide world—
Dad

Priorities Are Best Seen...
Not Talked About

Dear Kari, Lisa, and Julie,

Yesterday, I preached at church on Luke 9:25: "What good is it for a man to gain the whole world, and yet lose or forfeit his very self?" This verse challenges us to consider what we value most, and to ask ourselves the question, "To what should I dedicate my life?" Someone who lives only for all the things the world has to offer may, in the end, forfeit his very soul for eternity.

What will the man you marry most value? What will he live for, and what will be the greatest driving factors in his life? I have every confidence that each of you will marry Christians. But your mom and I spend most of our time counseling Christian couples, so we know that being a Christian does not inoculate you against having a diseased or troubled marriage. My prayer is that God will give you a man who lives his life with God-honoring priorities.

You might ask, "How can I know, before I am married, what a man's true priorities are?" At our weekend seminar for engaged couples, we always start with a game. We divide everyone into groups of three or four couples each and ask them to pretend that they are about to interview a candidate for the CEO position of a top company, or the manager of a professional ball team, or the pastor of a large church. The rules are that in only three minutes, you must write down all the questions you would ask, in a 30-minute interview, to help you make the best decision regarding this candidate. You may assume that the interviewee would answer all the questions truthfully but there would be no time to check references—you must make your decision regarding the candidate at the end of the 30-minute interview.

After the engaged couples have done this three-minute exercise, we ask them to repeat the process, but this time the interview questions are to pertain to choosing a lifetime marriage partner. The exercise is a lot of fun, but then we always end with the question, "If you could ask only *projective* questions such as 'After we're married, what would you like to do with your Saturdays?' or *reflective* questions such as 'What do you typically do with your Saturdays?'—which would you choose?" Certainly there is value in both kinds of questions, but we suggest that if you could ask only one kind, it should be *reflective*—because it really doesn't matter as much what you would *like* to do as much as what you are in the *habit* of doing. I will refer to this exercise again in future letters, but for now let me focus on its relevance to values and priorities.

How does the man you are involved with spend his money? Is he a saver, or does he spend it all keeping up his pride and joy—his car? Perhaps he really does have to work during a lot of the hours that you know he'd rather be with you, but to keep up on the payments for his Beemer, he simply has no choice.

"He really would like to spend more time with me, but on Saturdays he is always glued to his 48-inch screen watching sports."

"He's so great to be with because he is always there for me. He isn't materialistic like so many other guys—in fact, he doesn't have a steady job, so he can be with me all the time." (We will talk about being a provider in another letter.)

"He is so hot. He spends two hours each day at the gym, runs every morning, and plays basketball two nights a week—all so he can keep his gorgeous body in shape. And someday that body will be mine. He would rather be with me, but life is full of choices, and when we get married, taking care of his body will be well worth it."

"He is so smart! He gets A+ in all his classes. He usually studies until 2 am. I wish he had time to go to church with me, but I know this is an especially intense time in his life. He plans to be a brain surgeon. I can't imagine being married to a brain surgeon—I mean, I guess there's a lot of money in it. I'm sure there are times he'll not be home, but he tells me that nothing will be more important to him than our children and me after we are married."

The scenarios could go on and on, but I think you get my drift. You find out about a person's priorities and values by observing both the choices they have made and the ones they are making now. That does not discount the fact that God is able to change any of us. The point is, you don't want to risk living the rest of your life with someone you *hope* will change.

The question to ask is, "What good is it for a man to have a great car—have a 48-inch TV screen—be unemployed—be "hot"—be a brain surgeon—and not be doing the things that honor God in this life and demonstrate his relationship with Christ?"

Please hear me clearly: I am not saying it's *wrong* to have a Beemer, own a 48-inch screen, be "available", be "hot," or be a brain surgeon. What I am saying is if such things are the *driving force* now in the life of your man, you will likely not find him making you the high priority in his life, as God calls on husbands to do.

The converse of all this is true as well. If you find that the man you are involved with now seems to be committed first and foremost to honoring God with all aspects of his life and you see that his choices in life reflect the priorities of God, it is a very good thing.

The verse preceding Luke 9:25 is verse 24 (I'll bet you already figured that out). It says, "For whoever wants to save his life will lose it, but whoever loses his life for me will save it."

That verse is one of the paradoxes of life. When we focus on our needs and ourselves first, then in the end, we lose. When we focus on losing our lives for others and in the will of the Lord, we actually become who God desires us to be and we experience "life to the full" here on earth as well as the promise of eternal life.

I am so thankful and proud of each of you and the choices and priorities in your lives. I so wish for you to be married to someone who will share and celebrate those priorities.

Love, Dad

Does He Love God's Word?

Dear Kari, Lisa, and Julie,

Yesterday, one of the assistant pastors at church stopped to tell me he had referred someone to me: an 82-year-old man who was dating a 65-year-old woman. The reason for the referral was that the man didn't feel scriptures prohibiting premarital sex applied to him since he was 82 years old, not 16. I responded that this man should be especially concerned about obeying the laws of his Maker since he would most likely be meeting Him in the near future. In fact, at his age, he might meet his Maker while in the act itself!

As humorous and somewhat absurd as this may seem, it illustrates a point I want to address with you. (No, I am not writing to you about sex—but that will come.) I want to express my desire for you to marry a man who accepts God's Word as "the final answer" on all issues. I long for you to have a husband who has a high view of scripture.

Today at lunch, your mom was telling me about a woman who had dated non-Christian guys for many years, and subsequently made the decision to date only Christian men. The woman was therefore a bit shocked—and very disappointed—to discover there was little difference between the behavior of the Christian men she dated and those who had no relationship with Him. These "godly" men were somehow able to shelve their biblical convictions when it came to physical involvement in dating.

> Find a man that has such respect for God and His Word that he obeys God's Word at all costs.

You want a man who simply says, "Scripture says it, I believe it, that settles it." This presupposes, of course, that he is a man who studies scripture and who therefore actually knows what it says. Furthermore, he should be a man who studies God's Word on his own, not just to impress you or others. The Bible says, "out of the overflow of his heart his mouth speaks."[1] If his heart is fully devoted to God's Word, his actions will follow.

How do you recognize this characteristic in a man before marriage? Glad you asked! When discussing a particular subject, does he base his belief on God's Word, on what others say, or on what "feels right"? I remember talking to a man (whom I greatly respected) about a subject that was quite controversial in his church. The man told me that everything in him wanted to go with the popular view, except for one problem: scripture. This man based his view not on what culture said, nor even on what his colleagues said, but on what he believed scripture said.

Is your potential husband a man who obeys God's Word, even when it may cost him more financially? Does he obey God's Word when his emotions are saying something different? Does he obey God's Word when his hormones are raging? Does he obey God's Word in family relationships even when he has been wronged? You will never find a man who *instinctively* always does the right thing toward others or toward you. You *are* able to find a man that has such respect for God and His Word that he obeys God's Word at all costs. This will make it more likely that you have found a man who will honor you. After Jesus washed his disciples' feet he said, "Now that you know these things, you will be blessed *if you do them*" (italics mine).[2]

May God lead you to a man who is "blessed" because he knows God's Word and follows it fully. If this happens, you will be a blessed wife.

Love, Dad

Is He Glad to Go to the House of the Lord?

Dear Kari, Lisa, and Julie,

This past weekend, while speaking at a marriage conference, your mom and I spent three hours talking to a woman who married a man she had led to Christ a year before they got married. They have been married for a number of years now. She shared with us that she is pregnant. Normally, for a wife, pregnancy would be the source of unparalleled joy. For this woman, however, her joy was mixed with the sobering reality that her husband is not on the same page as she is spiritually.

She asked us about raising children. How will she and her husband give spiritual direction to their children if they are not in agreement? What about church attendance, since he rarely goes now? How will they deal with his negative view of the organized church? And what about prayer at meals, since he rarely prays?

As she left, your mom and I were overcome with sadness for her. Instead of looking forward with joy to raising a child in the fear and admonition of the Lord, she has fears about *how* to raise a child in the fear and admonition of the Lord.

I have written before about the importance of marrying a Christian and about what scripture has to say concerning being unequally yoked. In this letter, I am moved again to emphasize to you how very important it is to marry someone who is genuinely, *fully* committed to following Christ.

Don't get romantically involved with someone who is a new Christian without giving him ample time to "level out." *Make sure* that his interest in and commitment to growing in Christ is completely independent from his interest in you.

In the case of the woman we spoke to at the marriage conference, her husband would say he is a Christian, but that he simply doesn't care to attend church. He generally doesn't *like* God's family. I do understand that some Christians can be pretty obnoxious—becoming a Christian does not instantly and automatically make one behave like a saint. However, God's Word is very clear that we are not to give up meeting together.[1] It really doesn't have much to do with whether or not you like the people in the building—you are called to meet with them regularly.

So, is this guy you like a guy who is glad when they say, "Let us go to the house of the Lord,"[2] or is he generally sad or negative about it? Does he take the initiative to pray with you? How is he growing personally as a follower of Christ?

It really has little to do with whether he is a nice guy or not. The husband of the woman we talked to is a really nice guy. They have fun together as a couple. But that is not the issue. The issue is that they are not on the same page on one of *the most important* issues they face, namely: what are we going to do in order to raise our children to follow Christ?

Some would simply say that since he is not opposed to her praying or going to church, there should be no problem. But they are *wrong*. The reality is, children often drift in the direction of the *less* spiritually mature parent—especially when the one not interested in developing his spiritual life is the *dad*.

Again, may I ask you to look at the history of the man? In no way am I implying that God does not transform lives; however, in the parable of the sower, we know that some seeds sprout up quickly and then die because they never take root and are choked off by the cares of the world.[3] You should always give plants time to grow so you can see what kind of health they will exhibit and what kind of fruit they will produce.[4]

I love you each so very, very much!

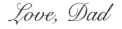

Love, Dad

Don't Marry out of Desperation or Pity

Dear Kari, Lisa, and Julie,

This past weekend, your mom and I had the privilege of speaking at a Valentine couples' dinner. Across the table from us was a couple who had been married for six months. Your mom started a conversation with the woman, and I with the man. On the way home, your mom commented what a delightful woman the young bride was and how vibrant she seemed to be in her faith. My conversation with the man, on the other hand, led me to think that he wasn't a believer. He talked about his wife being much more religious than he was and how his like for the pastor of their new church was such that he would now attend occasionally. I told your mom I was pretty sure the man did not have a personal relationship with Christ. She said I must be mistaken, since a woman who had such a vital faith would never marry a man who had none.

The very next day, our good friend Sue, who knew this couple, came over to the house to help us try to understand the computer world a bit more. Your mom asked Sue about their marriage. "He *is* a Christian isn't he?" But Sue confirmed he was not.

"How could she have married him?!" was our question. Sue said two very interesting things—first, that the woman was a real

45

"people pleaser." She didn't want to hurt anyone, and perhaps after getting involved with the man she was not willing to "break his heart" by breaking up, and so she married him. The second thing Sue said was that the woman felt she was getting older, and even though he wasn't everything he should be, perhaps "some man is better than no man at all."

Just the other week, your mom came across a saying that we both love: "It takes a great husband to be better than no husband at all." You might have to read that one a few times—I did. What it's saying is that it is better to be single than to be married to a man who is not right for you. In fact, a woman your mom counsels (who was recently divorced) begged her to tell all our Engaged Discovery Classes that the loneliest day of a single is better than being married to the wrong man.

Your mom and I have talked a lot about what would "make" someone marry a person who seems so clearly "wrong" for them. It may sound odd, but having parents with a "perfect" marriage might contribute to this poor choice. Some children have observed their parents having a wonderful marriage. This is good! But because of this, these children may feel that their own marriage will also automatically be wonderful. What they don't always take into account is the two individuals who contributed to the "wonderful" marriage. (I am so thankful I married your mom! I can't even imagine what it would be like to be married to a woman who was not passionate about family and ministry.)

Or, it could be focusing on the dream of "being married" rather than on *whom* one is marrying. Another way of saying this is that someone may be in love with love rather than in love with a specific person. Who doesn't dream of being married and living happily ever after? But what separates dreams from nightmares is largely one's choice of a spouse.

Or, it could be the example of parents who had a tough marriage but vowed—and kept their vow—never to divorce.

I once heard an engaged woman comment that her parents had said whatever happened in their marriage, they would not get a divorce. Since that had worked for her parents, she expected it to work for her, regardless of her trials in marriage. Certainly the commitment to stay married is commendable, but a marriage endured is not the goal. The goal is to have a marriage that thrives, not merely survives.

Sometimes an engaged couple will admit their relationship is really hard: "We argue a lot and we are very different in so many ways—but we will make it." I usually say, "Why? If you are having a tough time getting along during courtship, you will likely have a very tough time during your marriage." For most couples, the relationship moves along most smoothly and naturally during their courtship. They listen to each other, spend time with each other, enjoy getting gifts for each other, etc. Then, once they are married, the bumps and realities of life arrive. So, if their courtship isn't enjoyable, the likelihood is that their marriage will not be any better.

> It takes a great husband to be better than no husband at all.

Sometimes, someone desperately wants to start anew or get out of a very dysfunctional home situation. Again, the thinking is, *anything* will be better than staying at home. It may be true that getting away from home will be beneficial; however, trading one bad home situation for another will not necessarily prove to be heavenly—or even an improvement.

Well, our young bride made a huge mistake by marrying someone who did not share her faith. She also made the mistake of marrying someone who was a man *in* her dreams—but not the man *of* her dreams.

My prayer for you is that you will marry a man only if he is truly a great man. "Only a great husband is better than no husband at all."

Marry only great men, because you are great women.

I love you the whole wide world,
Dad

Character

The Four Seasons Rule

Dear Kari, Lisa, and Julie,

Recently, your mom met with a woman whom she had once counseled through a broken engagement. The woman had met a new man three months previously and was now announcing her new engagement. Instead of expressing delight, your mom, much to the disappointment of the woman, raised some concerns. Your mom's first question was how, after only three months, she was sure this was the "right" man. The woman assured your mom that this man was wonderful, a soul mate, and everything she had dreamed of. Your mom gently reminded her that three months into her previous relationship, she would have said all these things about her previous boyfriend. Yet now she "sees clearly" how wrong the first relationship was and how "perfect" this one is.

This letter is about what your mom has called the "Four Seasons Rule." This principle encourages couples to "go slow" and spend a long enough time together to really get to know each other. Why four seasons? Our experience has proved that in the rush to the altar many individuals do not get to know, as fully as they ought, the person with whom they are about to walk down the aisle.

Given a year's time, you will have the opportunity to see your young man in a variety of situations, and he will be able to do the same with you. Most couples in the early part of their relationship are caught up in the delight of being "in relationship." During these times they are more prone to overlook—or simply to not even observe—areas of weakness in each other.

I have a friend who loves to hunt. This creates some real tension in his marriage because his wife resents his being gone "with the guys." If you were to spend only three months getting to know such a man before committing to marriage, you might well miss the opportunity to observe his strong passion for hunting, the importance it plays in his life, and the way it occupies all his time, energy, and focus as the opening day of the season approaches.

Your mom has a friend who got married after a very short courtship. For this woman, birthday celebrations were *huge*. Unfortunately, she and her husband had not yet been together for her birthday. She was so disappointed when he did virtually nothing for her on her big day. It was not that he was a jerk—it was simply that he grew up in a family where birthdays were basically just another day of the year. He felt all the hoopla was a waste of time and money.

In some larger areas, also, you want to observe a man over the course of a full year. See how he reacts to his job. Is he stable in his work? How does he talk about his fellow employees or his employer? How does he deal with disappointment? How does he deal with conflict at work? How does he react during especially demanding times at work where he is required to put in, say, 12 to 16 hours a day for weeks on end to meet deadlines?

You want to see how he deals with holidays: is he a Scrooge or a Santa Claus? Does he love the holidays, or does he curse their arrival and celebrate their departure?

How does he interact with you when you are sick, a bit depressed, or simply not that fun to be around?

Someone once said to me, "Time is your friend." I think that is a great phrase. If a relationship is right for you, more time will simply confirm it. If you are afraid that more time will "hurt" your relationship, you should examine what is at the bottom of your fear.

Sometimes a couple will rush their decision because they want to honor God with their physical relationship and they feel they simply can't control themselves if they wait. I applaud their desire to remain sexually pure. However, I question the wisdom of rushing down the aisle so you can jump into bed. I certainly believe marital sexuality is a wonderful gift from God, but if it is the driving force to get married, it will likely need to be the driving force to keep the couple satisfied in their marriage. It has been our experience and observation

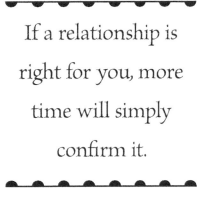

If a relationship is right for you, more time will simply confirm it.

that, as wonderful as marital sexuality is, it is not the glue that keeps marriages together. There are ways to "pace" your physical relationship so it does not become the impetus to a quick marriage. We will talk more fully about the subject of physical involvement in subsequent letters.

There are people who rush into marriage for "financial" reasons. If a couple rushes the process to "save money," they often find it very expensive to solve the issues not dealt with thoroughly before marriage.

We even know couples who get married "early" so they can be married in the place of their dreams. We counseled a couple who moved their marriage up six months so they could have the perfect setting for their wedding and reception. The beauty of that day faded quickly as they realized their dream wedding was turning into a nightmare marriage—because they had never really gotten to know each other.

Have I told you how much I love you and how I want each of you to marry the absolutely best man for you? Take your time; enjoy getting to know each other. You have your whole life ahead of you. My desire is for you to spend it with someone who will love and cherish you fully.

Love, Dad

He's Got to Leave
Before He Can Cleave

Dear Kari, Lisa, and Julie,

Last week, your mom and I spoke to a group of moms on the subject of "Healthy Extended Family Relationships." One of the women came to me afterwards to tell me her story. She said she really struggled with her in-laws and her husband's relationship with them. When she and her husband announced her pregnancy with their third child, her father-in-law lectured them about how they should have only two children, and has not talked to them since. The mother-in-law said she sure hoped they had a girl since their other two children were boys. When the woman and her husband called to say they had given birth to a third boy, the mother-in-law hung up on them. The in-laws have not visited the couple and their new baby in two months, even though they live in the area.

On a previous occasion, when her husband's parents were over for a visit, her father-in-law announced to the family that they were all going out to dinner. The woman (who at that time had just the two boys) said that it was nap time and so it would be better to wait and go out after the boys had had their naps. The father-in-law told everyone to get in the car—and they did. At the restaurant, the father-in-law seated himself and the rest of the family at one table and his daughter-in-law by herself at another.

The relationship a man has with his parents greatly affects the relationship he will have with his wife. Scripture says that a man should "leave his mother and father and cleave to his wife and the two will become one flesh."[1] As your mom and I have often said, "You can't cleave until you leave."

The leaving referred to is not simply a physical leaving. It has to do with the healthy separation of a son from his parents. The word "leave" in the Hebrew actually means to abandon, sever, cut off, forsake. The reason for this separation is to enable the new couple to cleave to each other more fully, to become one, and then to relate to their parents as adults rather than as dependent children.

Certainly part of this leaving has to do with financial independence. Is this man able to "pay his own way"—or have his parents always "taken care of him"? Is he able to make decisions that go against the wishes or advice of his parents? Is he emotionally dependent on pleasing them to the point of always building his future around decisions that will gain their approval?

Scripture is very clear about the responsibility of children to obey parents,[2] but adults are to *honor* parents, not obey them.[3]

I am not suggesting that you look for a man who never talks to his parents, has walked away from them, and has no relationship with them. Scripture is also clear regarding our taking care of our family. Sometimes this includes parents. We are to care for our parents—but not at the expense of our own marriage.

A close family can be both a blessing and a curse. A close family is a wonderful gift from God. I like to think of our family as a close family. It gives your mom and me immense joy to be with you and to know that you like to "hang out" with us. At the same time, I am thankful that you are each able to function apart from us. It is healthy that you don't need to call us daily and are able to make decisions on your own. In these past few weeks, for example, Kari has traveled to Jasper with friends and booked her own flight to visit a friend in St. Louis. Lisa has made decisions as an RA that show independence and maturity, and has managed her life with much grace. Julie is applying to colleges and universities without our assistance. We thoroughly enjoy any time we have to be with you or to talk with you—but are delighted that you don't "need" us to survive.

How might you know if the man you are involved with has a healthy relationship with his family? Consider how he talks about them. Is he respectful? Does he honor them even when he does not agree with them? Is he dependent on them financially? I realize that while in college, many students are dependent on their parents—so look for ways that he is moving toward financial independence. This is one reason we do not normally advise a couple to get married unless they have each lived away from home on their own for a while. I remember that after asking your mom to marry me, her father (your grandpa) asked me to give him an accounting of how I was going to support his daughter. I didn't have much money then, but I was employed, had been out on my own for three years, and was not financially dependent on my parents.

When your boyfriend is with his family, does he revert to being a child, or does he interact as an adult with his parents? Is he able to make decisions on his own? Is he willing to move away from the geographic area his parents live in? Does he feel the necessity to be with his family for the holidays? I am not saying it is wrong to be together for the holidays—far from it! I am simply asking whether he feels he *must* be with his parents.

You know that I came from a very close family. I am so thankful for the heritage that I received from my parents. I must tell you, however, that in the early years of our marriage, I was often more concerned about disappointing my parents than about hurting your mom. Part of the leaving is to have your primary allegiance changed.

Do you remember the story I told you at the beginning of this letter? It would be easy to be critical of this woman's in-laws, and rightfully so. Their situation does speak to the issue of marrying a family and not just an individual, but that is a topic for another letter. The real point of the stories I related is that the husband did not stand up to his parents to be an advocate for his wife. He should have said, "No, we are not going to dinner until the children have their naps." He should have said, "We will all sit at the same table, or in some other arrangement—but you are not assigning my wife to another table, or we are leaving." Instead, the husband was silent and allowed his wife to be deeply hurt. He said, in essence, "that's just the way my parents are, so get used to it." But his parents were wrong, and so was he.

I don't know what kind of a family you will marry into, but I do desire that you will marry a man who has left home in a healthy way, who will make you his priority, and who will make every effort to relate to his parents and to us in an adult-to-adult relationship. I so want you to marry a man, not a boy.

Love, Dad

How Important Is Your Family's Opinion?

Dear Kari, Lisa, and Julie,

It has been so good to be together for Thanksgiving on the farm these last few days. Last night, as we sang and shared together after dinner, I was again reminded of how blessed we are to be in an extended family where all your cousins love the Lord and each other. I delight in seeing how protective all the cousins are of each other in regard to any romantic relationships. It is a daunting task for any suitor to come under the Friesen cousins' scrutiny! It again reminds me of how important it is to surround yourself with people who know and love you and aren't afraid to speak truth about their observations to you when it comes to relationships.

Your mom and I have had conversations with two different couples in the last few weeks who have had less than supportive family input regarding their relationships.

One was a couple where the wife was upset with her husband because he'd decided to skip what she felt was an important commitment in order to please his family by meeting his aunt at the airport. As the wife was telling us how important she felt it was for him to keep his commitment, she slipped in the comment, "His family has never liked me anyway." We could see the pain on her face as well as the dilemma he found himself in as he was trying to meet the expectations of both his parents and his wife.

Another couple who spoke with us found themselves in a similar situation: his parents had disapproved of his fiancée and said they would not support the relationship. He had explained to his parents that he intended to marry this girl anyway, since he loved her and believed that the issues they raised were merely cultural and personal preference issues—not character or biblical issues at all. He did marry the woman, but it has cost him his relationship with his family; they no longer will talk to him. He and his wife, however, seem to be doing well.

There is certainly a lesson to be learned from these couples regarding the need to leave before you can cleave. However, because of our recent extended-family time together, I've been thinking more about the role one's family plays in the process of deciding whom to marry. I will admit from the start that I am very slow to cast an approving vote for any of your suitors. With that said, let me think with you about the role of family in your relationships.

First, there is no question that having a family with similar faith and values is a huge advantage to a relationship. Your mom was remarking to me on how each of your Clark cousins married into families of strong faith and what a blessing that has been for those marriages. I realize that not everyone falls in love with someone from such a family. There are certainly many examples of people from families of strong faith happily married to persons whose families have no faith; but generally, with such marriages comes a set of challenges one does not experience in families of like faith.

Second, your family is often a great source of good counsel regarding relationships, not only because they know you well, love you, and want the best for you, but because they are able to be a bit more objective in their observations.

Individuals with close relationships to their families find it extremely challenging to marry someone whom they know their parents don't approve of. (Part of the reason is that children will always yearn for their parents' approval and acceptance.) These individuals will tend to be less relaxed when with their parents because they are always conscious that their mates are being judged.

Such situations are also difficult for the spouses. Recently, we were visiting a couple who had been married for 30 years. The husband is an accomplished musician and a nationally recognized worship leader. The wife's family had never really accepted him because he didn't have a "real job." We were in their living room when the husband answered a call from his wife's parents. I will never forget the expression on his face when he got off the phone. His in-laws had invited him to minister at their church as a guest speaker. He looked at us and said, "For the first time in 30 years, I have felt their approval and acceptance of me." That is a long time to believe your wife's parents do not think you are good enough for their daughter.

A great gift to me throughout our marriage has been your mom's parents' acceptance of and love for me. I can't imagine what it would be like if they had never approved of me.

Third, there are times when, because of a different faith position, cultural perspective, or parental values (for example, "I raised my daughter to marry a minister!"), one may choose to marry without one's parents' blessing. This is a huge decision, but not necessarily always the wrong one. In those cases where parents don't agree with their child's choice of a mate, I would suggest that the young people pray for God to confirm His best in everyone's hearts. Always act in a respectful manner as you explain your case to your parents. Slow the relationship down a bit to give your family time to get to know and love your intended.

Finally, ask God to clearly show you His best and help you to be open to hearing the counsel of those who love you.

May God give you wise counsel, ears to hear it, and a heart to respond to it. Pray for me, too. Letting you go into the arms of another man is easier said than done!

Thanks for allowing me to wrap my arms around you all these years. Even more, thanks for welcoming the arms of the only perfect Father you will ever have, and for listening so beautifully to His voice.

I love you more than any other man has loved you thus far. Don't be too afraid. I *do* want to release you into the arms of another man... someday.

Love, Dad

Is He a Leader?

Dear Kari, Lisa, and Julie,

Last night, we were counseling a recently engaged couple. When we asked them about the level of their physical involvement with each other, the man said, "She has said 'no sexual intercourse before we are married,' and I am willing to honor her wishes." I looked at him and asked, "If she told you she loved you and, since you were planning on getting married, she wanted to have sex with you, would you?" He said, "Certainly, if it were OK with her."

I realized a number of things about the man that evening. First, he had a very low regard for God's Word and its clear directives regarding premarital sex. Second (and this is what I want to write to you about today), he was not leading. Two of the most common complaints we hear from wives are that their husbands are not "involved" and that their husbands don't lead. In the wonderful book *The Silence of Adam*, author Larry Crabb suggests that Adam and Eve were together in the garden of Eden when the serpent arrived.[1] The serpent approached Eve and engaged her in the conversation that culminated in her eating the fruit off the tree from which the Lord had told Adam they were not to eat. Crabb suggests that instead of entering into the conversation and "leading," Adam kept silent and "walked away."

In many homes, men have been walking away ever since. It is interesting to me to observe that although Eve was the first to eat the forbidden fruit, it is Adam who is held responsible throughout scripture: "Therefore, just as sin entered the world through one man..."[2] Throughout scripture, the leadership directives are given to *men*. Certainly there is partnership between husband and wife, and we are each responsible for our own actions. But somehow, in the economy of God, He holds men responsible to lead.

There is an interesting set of statistics from Promise Keepers that states, "If a child is the first to come to the Lord, 3% of the time the family follows. If the mom is the first to come to the Lord, 17% of the time the family follows. If the dad is the first to come to the Lord, 93% of the time the family follows." This in no way is saying anything disparaging about the role of children or mothers. It simply is reflecting the fact that fathers *do* lead—in one direction or another.

In his book *Iron John*, Robert Bly states that we have raised a culture of sweet and gentle men, but not many men who truly lead.[3] I would agree. As we work with couples, we see many husbands who, somewhere along the path, "dropped out." They became what I call "Yes, dear" men. Years ago, they quit being leaders in their homes. Instead of entering into constructive discussions when their wives didn't agree with them, they withdrew, feeling this was the way to "keep the peace."

What does this all have to do with you and the young man you might be interested in? You want to find a man who has strong, godly convictions and is willing to take the initiative in leading you into discussions regarding any decisions the two of you are making. Are you the one who always seems to come up with the ideas? Is his favorite phrase "whatever you want"? On the surface, this may seem like a wonderful attitude. "He doesn't care what we do, as long as it makes me happy." I would agree that you should want a man who is serving you and who is concerned for your happiness. But the "whatever you want" statement puts all the pressure on you to lead. It is now *your* responsibility to initiate. You might have the feeling that if *you* don't initiate something, the two of you will always end up staying home, or never enter into any meaningful service.

Instead of "whatever you want, dear," a man who is a servant leader might say, "I really hope we can spend some time together this weekend. I hear the weather is to be beautiful. I was thinking it might be a great day for a long bike ride. Does that sound good to you, or do you have another idea?" You might think that's merely a difference of semantics, but I don't agree. The latter set of statements would come from a man who is involved and taking initiative, but wanting to serve you at the same time.

Another way to identify leadership in a man is by how he treats you in the area of morality. Many couples will be involved physically until the point at which the woman says "stop." The next day, the woman may say that she felt they went too far physically the night before. The most common response of the man is, "Well, you didn't say 'stop.'" All too many men feel it is the woman's responsibility to lead in this area. Fast forward to marriage, and here is what likely will happen: Your husband will play golf every Saturday with the guys. When you finally say that you wish he would stay home with you and the kids, his response will be, "You never said you didn't want me to play golf." Or, he leaves for the office before the kids are awake and stays at the office late every night, coming home after the kids are in bed. One night you mention your concern that he is missing seeing the kids grow up—to which he replies, "You never said I should be home." The examples could go on and on, but the point is the same. In all these cases he expects *you* to lead.

You are all strong women with a real nurturing side. It would be all too easy for you to meet and start to care for a guy who is "so nice"—yet fail to notice that he is not going to be the partner in leadership you need.

We see many a woman whose father was aloof, non-affectionate, always at work, and driven to excel at everything—except being there for his girls. These women tend to be attracted to men who are not driven. Let me describe to you how it works. Daughter from "non-involved dad"-home meets man who adores her, always has time for her, compliments her, and is affectionate towards her. This feels wonderful to her. Finally! She has found a man who has time for her, is affirming of her, and is physically expressive. She may or may not realize that she is attracted to all she missed in a relationship with her dad. She marries Mr. Wonderful, and shortly afterward realizes why he always has time for her... because *he doesn't do anything*! She lives in a dump, because they can't afford anything else; she drives a car that barely runs; and she might need to go to work herself to provide food for this man who is always there for her... *on the couch*. She now starts thinking back to her childhood and living in a comfortable house with a car that runs and food that satisfies and realizes that Dad made that happen. I am in no way defending uninvolved dads; I am simply pointing out that many women let the pendulum swing all the way to the other side and miss out on marrying a man who is a servant leader with balanced, Biblical priorities.

Well, I rambled on a bit today. Seeing you enter this phase of life—where you are interacting with potential mates—may be the most challenging part of life so far for me. I so want you to marry men that will lovingly partner with you and lead in a God honoring way.

Love, Dad

Is He a True Servant?

Dear Kari, Lisa, and Julie,

As I was walking this morning, I was thinking how we used to sing the song "Make Me a Servant." I smiled as I thought of the revised lyrics we have sung to each other over the years when we wanted something done for us: "Make *You* a Servant."

As much as it brings a smile to my face, I am quite serious that the character trait of servanthood in a man is a critically important one for him to exhibit.

When the Apostle Paul wrote about marriage in Ephesians 5, he instructed men to "love your wives as Christ loved the church." This sounds like a reasonable directive. What new husband doesn't love his wife? Many husbands will reason that "Christ was the head of the church" means "I'm in charge." But the essence of this passage is that men are to treat their wives as Christ treated the church.[1] The truth of the matter is that Christ came to *serve* the church, not to be served *by* the church.

Whenever I am talking to men, I explain that the Biblical model of leadership is servanthood. A husband is not to be the "king of the castle," but the "servant in the castle." Certainly, we are *all* called to be servants, but if there is one person who is to be the chief servant, it is to be the husband.

For a wife to be served and cherished by her husband is critical for a vital marriage. Your mom and I ache to see so many wives who are married to men who put their personal interests ahead of their relationships with their wives.

So, the question is: how do you know, before marriage, whether a man will live out Jesus' model of servanthood?

You might be tempted to conclude that he is a good servant because he brings you flowers or does things for you. *Of course he does*—he's smitten with you! This may sound odd, but the way to see the character of a man is not just by observing how he treats you, but by observing how he treats those he is *not*

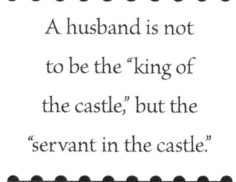

A husband is not to be the "king of the castle," but the "servant in the castle."

smitten with. There will be days in marriage where he is not smitten with you. Life will become routine, and he will return to his life patterns.

When a young man is at his home on vacation, does he help with domestic chores, or does he expect his mom to wait on him? Does he push for further physical involvement after you say no? Does he hop up to offer his seat to someone in need? Does he stay up late (or get up early) to help someone in need—even if it means sleep deprivation? When the platter of food is passed, does he take the best piece of chicken because he is first? Does he attempt to "cut people off" in order to get ahead on the freeway? Is he one of the first to volunteer when the call for helpers is given?

To have a man who, in the words of Philippians 2, considers others more important than himself, is a real gift.[2]

What happens when you marry someone who puts himself ahead of others in his marriage and in his family? He may play golf every Saturday because "I've worked hard all week and I deserve it." He may not help with domestic chores because "I'm tired and I've worked hard all day." He may always insist on going to *his* movies because yours are "chick flicks." He may quit his job because he "gets all the hard jobs." He may have an affair because he is not happy with you and claims "I have a right to be happy."

You will recognize servanthood if you look carefully. You want a man who loves to serve. This will not be difficult if you have a man who loves Jesus—because when one loves Jesus, one wants to be just like him. As John Ortberg said, "When Jesus came in the form of a servant, he was not *disguising* who God is. He was *revealing* who God is."[3]

I love you, girls, and I don't want you to be married to some selfish jerk who is "so hot" or "so funny" or "so rich" or "so nice" or "so much fun." Hot gets cold, funny gets old, rich gets poor, nice is not always so, and fun isn't all life is about. Marry a man who will cherish you and serve you all the days of your life.

I love you, girls, and want you to be treated as princesses— because that's who you are!

Love, Dad

A Selfish Mate Is Worse
Than No Mate at All

Dear Kari, Lisa, and Julie,

It has been so good talking to each of you this week and seeing how God is meeting you in this new academic year. Julie, it was especially fun to visit you at Cal Poly and see you in your new environment.

Your mom and I miss each of you, but we are so proud of you and thankful for who you are and for your hearts for Christ and His kingdom work.

This last week has been one of contrasts for your mom and me.

On Wednesday, I met with a man who told me he wasn't sure whether he wanted to stay married. He said he had a wonderful wife and two darling girls, but he really preferred being on the golf course or out drinking with his buddies rather than spending time with his family. I asked him if it had always been this way. He explained that before they had children, his wife "let" him do whatever he wanted. She also had a separate life, so he didn't think it seemed to matter much. He went on to say, "after we had children, she settled down and expected me to be home more. I really don't think I should have to be there, since I would rather be golfing. Do you think I am being selfish?"

"Yes, I do," I responded. I referred him to Matthew 19, where

Jesus says, "the two will become one...they are no longer two."[1] I suggested that he and his wife had never really become one. They had lived parallel lives as a married couple but had never "died to themselves" for the sake of their marriage.

I also gently suggested that he had really never grown up. Part of being a husband and father is doing the "adult" thing of putting the needs of those you love ahead of your own. He insisted that his own lifestyle was not "hurting" anyone. I suggested it *was*—and that it would continue to hurt his wife and his two children. If in fact it wasn't hurting anyone, why was he presently separated from his wife?

On a side note, when I asked about his and his wife's faith experience, he admitted that he had no current involvement in a faith experience, but that his wife did. How tragic yet common this scenario is!

Last weekend, we counseled a couple who were married while in their thirties. Their vocations were drawing them away from each other. Both were intent on pursuing their own vocational goals, even though it meant separation from each other for weeks at a time and put enormous strain on their marriage. The decisions they had to make would be difficult for any couple—but especially so for them, because their faith experiences were so very different from one another's. (Have I ever mentioned how critical it is to marry someone with a vital faith like your own?)

During a break that afternoon, we had lunch with Pete and Lynn, married only three weeks ago. They also were both in their thirties. During our conversation, they talked about their respective jobs and the adjustments they were facing as two singles coming together as one. Pete explained that he was now getting up at 5:30 AM each morning to begin his work day from home. That way he could wake up with Lynn and be "off" by the time she got home. Before their marriage, Pete would wake up late and work late. He made a significant adjustment so that their lives would be more in sync.

Within a span of 72 hours we had seen so clearly the difference a serving rather than a selfish spirit makes in a marriage.

You are all wonderful servants. Your mom and I talked about this as we watched Julie during her lacrosse practice. Julie was always one of the girls helping to carry the portable lacrosse goal whenever it needed to be moved during practice.

Serving others and putting their needs ahead of your own becomes a pattern, even in relationships. Certainly in marriage both husband and wife are called to serve each other; however, our observations tell us that more often than not, the serving spouse ends up serving alone—unless she (or he) also marries a dedicated servant.

> You are each princesses— daughters of the King—so make sure you marry a man who treats you as a princess and delights in serving you.

I so long for you to marry a man who is selfless rather than selfish. As you have heard me say before, "selfishness is the number one killer of marriages."

You are each princesses—daughters of the King—so make sure you marry a man who treats you as a princess and delights in serving you. I have no worry that each of you will serve your future husbands well.

Have I ever told you that serving you has been one of the

greatest privileges of my life as your father? It is still hard for me to believe that there is someone out there who will serve and cherish you well enough to satisfy me. I guess that's why God took on the responsibility of being the matchmaker instead of leaving it up to dads.

Love, Dad

Don't Assume
He'll Mature

Dear Kari, Lisa, and Julie,

Did you hear the one about how men and savings bonds are different? Savings bonds mature! As humorous as that may be, sometimes it's not funny at all. I believe it is very important to be satisfied with the man you marry *as he is*, and not expect him to change significantly.

At a recent Engaged Discovery Weekend, a woman referred to something that annoyed her about her fiancé, and then announced, "but I'll change that in him."

I don't want in any way to deny that we all change—and some of us actually do mature! I don't want to deny God's power to transform each of us into new creatures. But I do want to question the wisdom of entering a life-long covenant relationship with someone that you *hope* will change or mature. While you certainly need not declare each other "perfect" before you walk down the aisle, you should be *very satisfied* with the person you are marrying—without reservations.

You should not marry until you are relatively sure of the character of the one you are marrying. That is why many experts on marriage discourage couples from marrying until they are at least in their early to mid-twenties. The thought here is that by that time they should have leveled out and steadied a bit in regards to their direction and priorities in life.

This is part of the "leaving" in "Leave, cleave, and become one." You want to be sure that what you are left with is what you want to cleave to. Far too many women have gotten married— with hopes and promises—only to be greatly disappointed in the realities of good intentions with no carry-through.

In what areas should you look for maturity in a potential husband? Certainly, direction in life is one. I always love it when I ask a young man, "What do you plan to do with your life?" and, with passion, he lights up and starts to describe his plans for the future. On the other hand, I have definite concerns when after I ask that question the reply is, "I don't know, man, I'm just sort of waiting to see what turns up." This is the kind of guy you will most likely want to turn down.

Look for maturity in the area of responsibility. Is your friend generally irresponsible? He most likely will have that tendency the rest of his life.

Your mom has surely told you how neat my apartment always looked whenever she visited me. She now says she was misled, because she never saw my bedroom—or the other areas of the apartment where I had simply thrown stuff before she arrived. Does that mean that if your mom had seen my bedroom, we would not be married today? You'll have to ask her that one! But, clearly, if she had known of my sloppy ways, she would have been better prepared to deal with what has turned out to be an area of tension in our marriage—or she might have decided it was a tension she was not willing to live with. I was, am, and always will be "neatness-challenged." I work on it, but it's an area I will never "mature" in fully.

Some guys are lazy. Their fiancées cater to them, expecting that they will mature and become productive after marriage. We have seen many marriages where the male was unemployed prior to marriage, but promised he would get a job after marriage. Savings bonds mature, but some men don't!

A lack of maturity might exist in an area as simple as personal hygiene or manners. You certainly don't want to be a "mother" training your "little boy" to act maturely.

Too many times, when we ask women why they married their husbands, they answer, "He was so good looking" or "He was so funny" or "I just loved him" or "He was so sweet." There is nothing wrong with being good looking, funny, lovable, or sweet. (Well, maybe not "sweet"—you know how I feel about that!) I trust you will find a husband who is a man of character, direction, and integrity. I wish for you a man who is kind and serving, who loves and serves the Lord fully. These characteristics should be evident *now*—not a dream for the future.

I don't really care a whole lot about what your future husband will *do* for a living, but I deeply care about who he will *be*.

Have I ever told you what a huge decision this is? I sure do love you girls—and I want for each of you someone who will love you at least as much as I love you. Remember that past performance is worth far more than future promises when it comes to investments—and marriage.

Love, Dad

What's His
Self-Control Quotient?

Dear Kari, Lisa, and Julie,

During my quiet time this morning, I was reading chapter two of the New Testament book of Titus. I was struck by the lists of instructions given there to older men, to younger men, to older women, and to younger women. The common instruction for each group was to learn *self-control.*

This letter is a bit harder for me to write because self-control is something I have struggled with my whole life. This is no secret to you, but I regret not having modeled a Christ-like lifestyle in this area. My struggle for self-control is most obvious in my weight. I have not controlled my eating—and it has shown. I wish eating were the only problem, but I find the lack of self-control permeates many areas of my life: my personal spiritual disciplines, my exercise disciplines, and others.

My current practice is to get up at 5 am each morning to read a Psalm, then a Proverb, an Old Testament chapter, a New Testament chapter, and then a reading from Oswald Chambers[1]—followed by prayer. After that, I take the dog out for a run/walk and then have my "Zone meal." Following this routine, I am amazed at how much better I feel about myself—how much better I feel physically, how much more energy I have. It makes me wonder, "Why don't I *always* live this way?" The answer is: because I have chosen to let life control me instead of me controlling my life. As the Psalty song we sang so many times while you were young says, "Self-control is just controlling yourself."[2]

I am thankful for how each of you have chosen to live lives of self-control. I am so thankful for the discipline I see in your spiritual, physical, and eating habits.

How can lack of self-control affect a marriage, and how do you recognize this problem in a man you are dating? Proverbs 25:28 says, "Like a city whose walls are broken down is a man who lacks self-control." The picture this paints for me is a city that is vulnerable to all sorts of attacks because it has no defenses in place. Once the enemy is on its way in, it's a little late to start building.

Lack of self-control in marriage is expressed in a variety of ways. It can sometimes be expressed through laziness. A man who has little self-control is seldom motivated to do those things that are difficult. He will often choose sitting on the couch watching TV over working in the yard. A man lacking self-control will often spend money without careful thought. A man lacking self-control will often eat whatever is appealing without asking what is healthy. Often a man without self-control will have more difficulty in keeping his mind pure. A man with little self-control is more susceptible to affairs after marriage.

On the other hand, a man who exhibits self-control will more likely be willing to do unpleasant tasks, watch over your money carefully, watch what he eats, keep his mind pure, and remain faithful to his wife.

How can you tell whether a guy has a problem with self-control? Some things are obvious. I lost 30 pounds before getting married. I was not going to be naked and fat on my wedding night! This did demonstrate that I could be disciplined enough to lose weight. What your mom failed to see was that it also said my habit *pattern* was not one of self-control in this area.

You may be wondering whether I'm suggesting that your mom should not have married me because she saw I struggled in this area. No—but I *am* saying that awareness of this character deficiency should be factored into your decision about whom to marry. I would like to believe I have other qualities that offset this deficiency—however, I am aware that my lack in this area has detracted from the relationship we could have had if I had been more disciplined.

> A woman who tries to control or change her husband is seldom successful and usually is met with resistance.

OK, back to how one can recognize lack of self-control in another. There are skinny men who are not self-controlled. Some can eat anything they wish and still stay thin. Others struggle with self-control in less visible areas.

When faced with the choice of watching TV or studying, does he have enough self-control to turn off the tube? When choosing between staying up late or getting needed sleep, does he exhibit self-control? When passing a rack of sexually explicit magazines does he walk on by—or take a look? When he could get a laugh by insulting someone, does he let the opportunity pass rather than hurt another? In your physical relationship, does he exhibit self-control—or does he push your boundaries?

One other thought before I close: if you marry a man with little self-control, you may find yourself trying to engineer "spouse-control." But a woman who tries to control or change her husband is seldom successful and usually is met with resistance.

In this area, as in so many others, recognizing and noting past behavioral patterns in a potential husband is more important than simply looking at his present performance.

I am sorry for the times I have hurt or embarrassed you because of my lack of self-control. I wish for you a man who is stronger in this area than I have been. I love you all more than you will ever know—and want you to marry a man who will behave responsibly and serve you.

Love, Dad

I'm Glad He Loves Jesus, but Does He Have a Job?

Dear Kari, Lisa, and Julie,

This week in the college group at camp, we asked what people would do if they were paid $125,000 a year to do anything. One young man answered, "I just want to serve Jesus." That sounded like the "right" answer to him—like that boy whose Sunday school teacher asked him, "What is about a foot long, has a bushy tail, and stores acorns in the winter?" The boy thought for a while, then said, "It sure sounds like a squirrel, but I'll say 'Jesus.'"

Serving Jesus is a wonderful and right thing to do, but along with that I wish for you a man who has a passion about a direction in life as well. So many men today are like the groom at the altar to whom the minister said, "It's 'I do,' not 'whatever'!" I am seeing far too many men who have no real direction in life, no call, and no passion. Your mom and I really don't care what the vocation of the man you marry is, but we deeply desire that he be passionate about *something*. No matter what his vocation, we trust his deepest passion will be to be a light for Jesus—but also that he will be involved in a life work that has meaning.

As a father, I want you to have a husband who is a good provider. You know me and our life experience enough to know that

I am not talking about a man who will necessarily be wealthy. I am speaking very clearly, however, about a man who provides for you so you will not be required to be the provider for the family nor needed to supplement the family income. I firmly believe that men are wired to be the providers and protectors of the family. When a man does not fulfill this part of his created image, he becomes less than he should be and will ultimately be frustrated with who he has become.

I certainly am not talking about "crisis" situations brought about by injury, layoff, or sickness. What I am talking about is a lifestyle that becomes dependent on your working. At your age, one of the situations that frequently arises is paying for continuing education. It is not wrong to help support your family for a short season; however, even in the area of education, I would not want you to be married to someone who expected you to "put him through." If he is not able to step up to the plate and work at least part time to help support his family while in school, I would be concerned about the type of man you have. You girls all have servant hearts and are very capable. I could see you each being willing to "support" a husband while he pursues his dreams. But sometimes a man's dreams become a woman's nightmare when not rooted in reality.

Let me give you an illustration that wouldn't be out of the realm of possibility for any of you: suppose you meet a man who loves God and says he wants to go into ministry when he graduates. You are excited, because God seems to be calling you this way as well. He realizes that seminary is a necessary step if he is to go into the ministry, so he asks you if you will support him until he gets his degree in three or four years. You work full time, he goes to school full time. You seldom see each other because of the demanding schedules you are both under. At graduation, you are elated. He has his degree! But, he has no experience, and the only job he can get to start is with a small church that can pay only $25,000 a year. So, once again you are working. Family? Not yet, because you need to work! Of course, you could always put the children in child care and pay someone else to be the primary shaper of your child's values...

My point is: marry someone who presently shows he will assume the primary responsibility to be the provider. You are able to see whether he is willing to work hard or will expect you to put in "equal time." Be leery of someone whose parents are willing to "help you out" so you can get through school. I am not against parents' generosity, but I *am* against parents continuing to provide for their children after those children have "left" home. If you don't truly leave you will never fully cleave.

Your grandpa Friesen moved to the farm in Pixley after being exhausted by many years of ministry. He had expected that the farm would give him more time for his family and would allow him to slow down from the hectic pace he had been keeping in Southern California. It was not long after their move, however, that he realized the farm, in its undeveloped state, would not support our family. Instead of insisting that your grandma work outside the home, he took a second job. There were times when his provision was only a little more than rice and beans, but he did provide—and mother was always at home for us.

Find a man who will provide for you.

The second reason I want you to marry a man with passion for his direction in life is so that he will be energized by what he does. Someone has said that 80% of Americans are working in jobs they don't like. I remember a friend of mine who taught school for 30 years and retired as soon as possible. He put in only the minimum amount of effort necessary and came home each day as early as he could. When he retired, he moved to the forest—because he had always really wanted to be a forester, but his parents had told him to be a teacher. As John Ortberg has said, "How sad to live your life only to look back and think what could have been." A man who is working in the area of his gift-edness and passion will be a much more vital man to live with. A man who is working in an area that is not his gift and passion will slowly die—and dead husbands are a drag.

Can you find this out before marriage? Glad you asked! What is his passion in life? Is he involved in something of value? Does he have a plan for his life? Is he intentionally working toward a goal? Is he presently working or involved in ministry—or is he just "hangin' around"? How does he spend his summers? How does he spend his vacations? How does he spend his free time? What does he talk about that he hopes to do? Is he presently doing anything in those areas to learn whether he is gifted in them?

My young college friend from camp loves Jesus—and loves to sit and play the guitar. I want you to marry a man who loves Jesus. I wouldn't mind if he played the guitar. But I do want to know that he is pursuing something in life that will use his passions to glorify God and to provide for my daughter. I don't want *you* working while he "trusts Jesus" and hopes that some-one will toss a few coins into his guitar case.

Have I told you girls how much I love you? Do you know how hard it is to think of someone else being your primary provider and protector? Do you see why I am slow to say "hooray" when you bring a new boy my way? I want you to marry a man—with a plan!

I love you—
Dad

Don't Marry
A "Crude" Dude

Dear Kari, Lisa, and Julie,

Yesterday, your mom and I were counseling a woman contemplating divorce. She was explaining the inappropriate behavior her husband was showing towards other women. When we asked if she had observed examples of this before she was married, she told us a story: While they were still engaged, they were at a buffet with some friends. One of her girlfriends was going through the buffet line in front of her fiancé. The girlfriend accidentally got some whipped cream on her hand and made some remark. The fiancé said, "Why don't you spread it over other parts of your body, and I could lick it off?" At this point in the story, the woman in our office exclaimed, "And this was before we were married! *What was I thinking?!* I can't believe I didn't see who he really was."

That conversation sparked two thoughts I want to share with you today.

First, being "male" is no excuse for being crude. I will write in a future letter about how God has wired us differently sexually. However, our wiring is never an excuse for sinful actions. Some men will respond, if challenged about a remark such as the one in the "whipped cream" story, that they were just joking. But there is a real difference between appropriate humor and what scripture would call "coarse joking."[1] May I suggest that such "joking" and coarse humor come from a deeper, more serious source? That source is one's heart. Scripture tells us that those things that come out of our mouths come from our hearts.[2]

Perhaps it is because your mom and I see so many women with husbands who have been unfaithful that I am so sensitive to this. Perhaps it's because you are my daughters and I want to protect you from someone who has a heart that is not fully devoted to the Lord.

Does the man you are with joke about sexual things? Do you see him lingering over pages in magazines that are sexually suggestive? Does he seem to stare at attractive women? When challenged, does he defend himself by saying, "Lighten up—all I'm doing is looking!" or "Hey, I'm a male; that's what males do"?

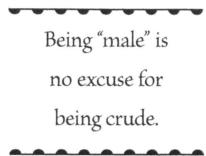

Being "male" is no excuse for being crude.

The woman we were counseling related to us a number of examples of instances in which her husband had spoken and acted in ways that were sexually inappropriate. *How surprising!* It is often in our humor, in our time together alone, or in private moments that our real character does come out.

The second thought our conversation with the woman highlighted is that it's never too late in a relationship to do the right thing.

One of our friends (whom you know) whose marriage ended in divorce told us that the night before she married her high-profile "very godly" fiancé, he became angry with her and continued to shout, "F— you, f— you, f— you!" She was stunned. But largely because of her own past and her self-image, she believed it must have been her fault—and so she went ahead with the wedding. Hindsight is always 20/20, but she should have called it off, or at least postponed the marriage.

I trust you will never be in either of the situations I have mentioned above. But I want you to know: if you discover at any time that you are involved with someone you have doubts about, pull out.

Your mom and I would much prefer some embarrassment and financial loss to having you enter a marriage that is not God's best. I remember with humor the prom one of you went to—with someone you barely knew. When you told your mom and me you had said "yes" and we asked you why, you said, "it was too awkward to say 'no.'" Later we laughed about the night, saying that perhaps a few minutes of "awkwardness" on the phone would have been better than an evening of misery at the prom.

May God protect you from intentional or unintentional impostors, and may you marry the real thing: a true man.

Love, Dad

One… (No Longer Two)

Dear Kari, Lisa, and Julie,

Well, today all of you, including mom, are on the West Coast enjoying the warm weather while I am holding down the fort here on the East Coast in 20-degree weather. Kari, enjoy San Diego for us; we love it there. Julie and Lisa, enjoy your time with your mom.

I wrote you a while back about the importance of being "whole" as an individual before you enter into marriage. The passage that I think I referred to was the Matthew 19 passage where Jesus is questioned about relationships and says that the two will become one.[1] My point in that letter was to emphasize that marriage is not the "completer." Our completeness must come from Christ and not from another person. Two *wholes* become one, not two *halves* become one.

The reason I am thinking about this today is that I am separated this week from your mom while she is out west with you.

The verse I mentioned goes on to say, "the two become one, they are no longer two." The mystery of marriage is that two do become one. I have mentioned before that we are complete before marriage. Yet, in a sense, after "the two become one," neither is any longer complete without the other.

I certainly am not talking *theologically*, as in our relationship with Christ. Even as married couples, our individual completeness still comes from Christ. Relationally, however, there is a real sense that when we are apart from each other, we are not "really whole." This is how I feel when your mom and I are apart for any amount of time.

After that long introduction, on to the main thought of this letter!

When scripture says, "the two become one, they are no longer two," it is a statement of the new priority of the marriage relationship over the desires and agendas of the individual. Many individuals today see marriage as an "add-on" to their lives rather than "new construction." Their mindset is that they will continue to live their lives as individuals and will simply now share a house and bed.

Let me give you an example from one couple we counseled. As a single, he had always had the guys over for Monday night football. After marriage, he simply told his wife that the guys would be over for dinner and football every Monday night, so if she wanted to leave the house and do something else that night, it was fine with him.

I am not saying that after marriage a husband may not watch Monday Night Football with the guys. What I am saying is that all such decisions are to go through the marriage grid, because "they are no longer two."

Another example from a more "spiritual" couple: they each taught Sunday school every Sunday, had individual Bible studies with their small groups each week, and were involved in different ministries—she in women's ministry, and he in men's ministry. After marriage, they decided they should attend a couple's Bible study each week as well.

Again, it isn't that ministry is "bad," but they had clearly just blindly tacked on the couple's Bible study (since "that's what Christian couples do"), adding to an already full week—rather than thoughtfully considering all their activity choices in the light of their new union, putting them all through the "what is best for our marriage?" grid.

I have written before how important it is to marry someone who is motivated and has a passion for what he does. I still believe in the importance of that. But where there could be an issue is when his passion for his work becomes more important to him than his passion for his marriage. His own agenda should not be more important to him than your shared agenda as a couple.

We also see this in the area of finances. More and more couples have each had their own jobs prior to marriage and have enjoyed their own independent lifestyles financially. Many couples carry this over into marriage and have their own checking accounts, savings accounts, etc. They divide up the family expenses but pay for them as individuals.

I remember a married couple who were hardly talking when they came in to see us. The issue that had caused so much tension surrounded an anniversary weekend away. She was very upset because he had not paid for dinner. She said, "I paid for the bed and breakfast, the least you could have done was pay for our dinner." He responded, "I just paid for the car repair by myself, so I didn't have money left over." This went on, back and forth, as they each explained what they had paid for. After a while we said, "Aren't you two married? Aren't your finances all together?" This is an example of a couple where the two became one legally, but were still two practically.

Observe whether your date's decisions are being governed by what is best for the *two* of you, or whether he tends to make unilateral decisions based on *his* desires. When the two of you want to watch different TV shows, is the solution "we'll both watch what we want on our own TVs"? If you can't decide what to do together for a weekend, is the solution "we'll each do our own thing and meet up later"?

I am not saying you can't ever go do something alone or watch your favorite TV show. But what you do want to look for is a spirit of willingness to put all activities and decisions through the grid of what is best for your relationship.

He may earn the money in the family, but the decisions are family decisions. Just last week we met with a couple where there was tension over how the money was spent in the family. She was a stay-at-home mom and he worked in the marketplace. The wife said, "Well, I guess he should be able to spend it like he wants since it's *his* money." We said, "Hello, it is *your* money just as much as his. The two have become one!" The "one" should make the financial decisions regardless of who brings home the check.

Certainly you are not one prior to marriage, but through discussions and observations you should be able to discern whether this is a "they are no longer two" man or a "they are still two" man.

I really miss your mom this week. I can function OK without her, but the truth is, "we are no longer two." I wish for you this same joy of always longing to be one again.

Love, Dad

Does He Have an "Entitlement" Attitude?

Dear Kari, Lisa, and Julie,

It is hard to believe that another summer is over. I am so thankful for each of you and for the way you serve so unselfishly each summer at the family camps we run. I especially appreciated the leadership each of you took in your various areas of ministry this summer. I know I am a bit prejudiced—however, I can't imagine a better trio to help model for young ladies what it means to grow into lovely women who love God and live life fully.

Last week at Lake Winnipesaukee, I went to our speaker's cabin to say goodbye to Bob and Carol Kraning. I walked in and noticed that instead of a double bed in their cabin, they had two twin beds. I still don't know how they ended up with that cabin for the week, but they never said anything to me about their accommodations. Bob and Carol easily could have complained about their cabin, especially since they were the guest speakers. Instead of complaining, they ministered to us in marvelous ways.

As I left their cabin last Friday night, I was so impressed with their character and lack of an "entitlement" attitude. I trust that one of the character traits *missing* in the man you marry will be that of "entitlement."

The attitude of "entitlement" puts a person outside the ordinary rules and norms of life. Entitlement people will often have a reason why the rules don't apply to them. They will often ask for special privileges because of their positions, etc. In the end, an entitlement attitude is an attitude of selfishness.

It can be as simple as talking at camp while someone is making announcements, or requiring special seating at a concert because of "who you are." In essence, an entitlement person says, "I am more important than others are. I deserve to get a better seat, not have to wait in line, not have to park in the 'regular' spots," etc.

This can cause significant issues in marriage for a number of reasons. First, if you are married to a entitlement man, he will be the entitled one and you will most likely be the one who is taken for granted or taken advantage of.

Secondly, if you are not an entitlement person, it will be very awkward since you will often be together. You may feel that waiting in line is what you should do, while your husband will feel no qualms about "pulling rank" to get special treatment.

Thirdly, if you have children, the attitude of entitlement will be modeled for them. There is little more irritating than entitled, spoiled children, who have been taught that life should revolve around them.

As I have said before, the attitude and actions of the man in the family really set the tone for the entire family. Certainly, because of the position or status of your husband, you may all be able to sit in better seats at a game, drive a nicer car, or have a deluxe room in a hotel—but a place of privilege is not "something to be grasped."

There is no question that Philippians 2 most clearly describes the attitude and actions of the only one who could ever rightly have an entitlement attitude: Jesus Christ. "Who being in very nature God, did not consider equality with God something to be grasped, but made himself nothing, taking the very nature of a servant...."[1]

If I had been the one assigning housing, I would have given the Kranings one of our better cabins. It is appropriate to honor those who preach the Word. But such honor is to be *given*, not grasped or expected.

I long for you to find a man that has an attitude like Bob and Carol's—an attitude like that of Christ. When you find such a man, you will find a man who is fully aware of who he is—just as Christ fully knew who He was—yet finds his significance not in where he sits, but in Whose he is.

I have seen how willing you all are to accept the servant's place. I deeply appreciate that and trust you will someday each be married to a man of God who will also find great joy in putting the interests of others above his own. Certainly a man like this will put the needs of his wife ahead of his own, and that makes me very glad.

You are not entitlement women. Make sure you each marry a man who is not an entitlement man.

I love you all more than you will ever know,

Dad

What Kind of Dad
Will He Be?

Dear Kari, Lisa, and Julie,

One October day in 1975, I was driving along Highway 8 in San Diego, California, thinking about Virginia and other girls I had dated in previous years. I certainly was no Casanova, but I had dated a bit.

The thought that I was pondering that day regarded motherhood. I remember thinking that while a number of the girls I had dated might have made good wives, no one could compare with your mom as I thought of who would be a wonderful wife and excellent mother. I have made a lot of wrong judgments regarding people over the years; however, I am thankful to say that my evaluation of your mom was right on.

I love the proverb "The apple doesn't fall far from the tree." This has certainly been true with each of you. I am so thankful I married such an incredible "tree."

Now, I am sure you can attest to the importance of a good father in the lives of his children. I have tried to be a good father and I believe, by God's grace, I have done an adequate job. Your mom and God have filled in where I have been less than I should have been.

It doesn't take a rocket scientist to see the incredible value of a strong father in the lives of children. Many studies affirm the importance of an involved father. Therefore, as you think of who might be a good husband, don't forget to think also of who might make a good father for your future children.

I am reminded of a man who once met with me who was contemplating divorce because he didn't like having children. He said they were not as much fun as his friends. He also complained that his wife was not as available and as carefree as she had been before they had children. What did he *think* would happen when they had children?

His wife should have picked up on this before their marriage, noticing that he was interested only in what brought him pleasure, on his terms and in his time. Apparently she hoped he would grow up—but he didn't.

Is the man you are involved with one whose character you want modeled for your children? Does he play well with children, or does he ignore them? Will he lead them toward the Lord? Is he one who puts others' interests before his own? Will he support your desire to stay home and care for the children, even if it means having less or his working more? How will he discipline the children? Will he be a fun father? Will he take them on special outings? Is he short-tempered? Will he choose to take care of the children so you are able to "get away" occasionally?

I wish for you a husband who will be a wonderful partner in parenting.

3 John verse 4 states, "I have no greater joy than to hear that my children are walking in the truth."

Thanks for giving your mom and me such great joy. I pray that God will give you each a husband who will partner with you in joy as you raise the children God may grant you.

Love, Dad

Considerations

I Hope He Knows How to Have Fun

Dear Kari, Lisa, and Julie,

Do you remember the one about the mushroom who went into a bar and sat down to order a drink? Apparently, the bartender came over and refused to serve him, saying, "We don't serve your kind." To which the mushroom replied, "Why not? Can't you see I'm a Fun-gi?"

Well, the reason for this story is certainly not to encourage you to take up any involvement with mushrooms, but with "fun guys!" Laughter and fun are so important in a marriage. Scripture says that a merry heart is good medicine. I think that means that fun makes you well.

Your mom is really often more fun than I am. (I used to be more fun, but life has unfortunately taken some of that away.) I remember dating your mom and all the fun we had. I will never forget our first "real date." I had sent her a written invitation asking her to dine with me in the finest ambiance in San Diego, with the most spectacular views. We would be eating the finest food, be entertained by the finest music, and enjoy it all with the finest company. Dress would be semi-formal. OK, so the "finest food" and "finest company" was a bit of a stretch. I showed up to pick her up in my '55 Ford station wagon, in 1974! I was dressed in my finest turtleneck sweater and sport coat.

The big evening arrived, and she came down to meet me—wearing one of the ugliest dresses I have ever seen! It did not fit well and, shall we say (kindly), it was *not* flattering. Turns out she thought it would be fun to see my reaction. I, being much more experienced in such expressions of humor, took it in stride and, calling her bluff, said, "You look beau-

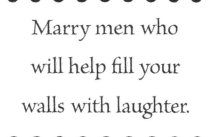

Marry men who will help fill your walls with laughter.

tiful! Shall we go?" Of course, she would not go out looking like that, so she went back to her room and changed. I then drove her to Sunset Cliffs, overlooking the Pacific Ocean. There, I set up a card table on which, while listening to background music by the Carpenters, we ate the lasagna dinner I had prepared.

On another occasion, we discussed the fact that we shouldn't be tying up her family's phone with our long, late-night phone calls. The next morning at 3 am, my phone rang. It was you-know-who, being "considerate" about prime time phone use.

Another favorite of mine is the time I made ham and cheese sandwich for a picnic lunch and purposely left the plastic wrapper on the individually wrapped cheese—so I could see her reaction as she bit into it.

I could go on and on. Suffice it to say, your mom and I have had many times and many years of fun and laughter together. I fully realize that some couples will be more serious than others. However, knowing you, I predict you'll each need someone who loves to have fun. Actually, I believe all couples need to have fun together in *some* way. Part of the reason I feel this way has to do with the state of the world: there are so many tragic things going on that one could get overwhelmed with gloom if it weren't for lighter times.

Consider also the thought of raising children in an atmosphere void of laughter and fun. Remember the difference Sister Maria made in the von Trapp home versus the atmosphere there with the Baroness Schroeder?[1] I long for the three of you to have homes with "laughter in the walls."

Jesus says in John 10:10 that he has come so that we might have life "to the full."[2] I certainly don't think Christians need to be giggling all the time; however, there is something about joyfulness that sounds *fun*. As our friend Ray Johnston says, "If you have the joy of the Lord in your heart, would you mind notifying your face?"

Speaking of Ray, it was also he who said he believed that the number one reason teens with Christian parents choose not to follow Christ is that they look at their parents and say, "I sure don't want to be like that when I'm older!"

I am so thankful that the walls of our home are filled with laughter. I wish for you to marry men who will help fill your walls with laughter as well.

Love, Dad

Frankly, I'm Crazy Enough Without the Bottle

Dear Kari, Lisa, and Julie,

I received an e-mail from a friend yesterday, expressing concern about a couple in leadership in their church and their involvement with alcohol. Apparently, a few times a year they go to places like Vegas with their friends and basically get plastered for the weekend.

I have thought before about writing you about men who drink, but stopped myself, because there are so many Christians who "drink responsibly"—and I realize that just because your mom and I don't drink doesn't mean *no one* should drink. I also realize that scripture does not forbid believers from drinking, so who am I to caution you about marrying a man who drinks?

I'll tell you who I am: I'm your dad who loves you "the whole wide world" and doesn't want to see you hurt by a man who allows alcohol to influence him negatively and thus hurt you and your children (our grandchildren)—should God grant you children.

Since I have now started on this subject area, allow me to continue and express myself honestly (as if you thought I wouldn't!).

First, you have all been raised without alcohol in your home and have expressed the desire that alcohol not be part of your married life. That is reason enough for a man to stop drinking for the rest of his life. If something is that important to you, and he is not willing to give it up entirely, then he is not a man who loves you fully. We have met with couples where the woman came from an alcoholic family that was extremely dysfunctional and who saw alcohol lead to abuse in her home and ultimately her parents' divorce. In one specific incident, a woman asked her husband please not to drink at home, but said it was all right while he was away. I appreciated her wanting to accommodate her husband, but in the end, he didn't want her to dictate his drinking habits. "After all," he said, "you knew I drank when you married me."

It is reported that 95% of date rape involves alcohol. Let me talk to you very directly as a male. When a man is with a very beautiful woman (such as each of you are), he is usually sexually attracted to her. He may be thinking that he would like to go to bed with her, but he knows her stand and has enough self-control not to force himself on her. But put alcohol into the equation, and his self-control is greatly diminished.

Isn't it interesting how often women at a party will have a drink so they can relax more and not be so inhibited? Perhaps, in fact, God designed us specifically to be inhibited—and alcohol dulls those God-given senses.

I also think of the complex issues involved with raising children in a home with alcohol. It may be one thing to say, "I drink responsibly"—but who is to insure that your son or daughter will?

Often men who become enraged do so after being influenced by alcohol. Once alcohol is a part of one's lifestyle, it is much more apt to be abused than if it were not part of the home at all. I can tell you that I will never be an alcoholic—because I will not take a drink. (Likewise, Julie will never get a sugar high—or low—because she eats no candy. I, on the other hand, have been known to gulp down multiple Snickers bars in times of stress or frustration.)

You know I could go on, and I know you know my heart, so I will not write much more.

I have no worry that you will ever bring a party animal home as your next boyfriend. I do want to caution you about marrying a man who does not share your viewpoint on this subject. Alcohol has brought great sorrow to many, many people.

Crazy enough without the bottle,
Dad

Do You Both Have Similar Passions?

Dear Kari, Lisa, and Julie,

It has been so good to be with you at camp again this summer. I love watching you work with children and marvel at your energy as you play with them during your "off" time. I am proud to be known as your dad as I see the girls flock toward you to hang out with you anytime they can. There is no time I see your passions so clearly demonstrated than when you are with the youth at Family Camp. Someday, most likely, you will not return to camp for the summer as you pursue other vocational avenues. My prayer for you is that you will always be able to live passionately as women of God, using the gifts God has given you to their highest and best purpose.

As I think about your future and your passions, I try again to imagine what kind of man you will marry. Have I ever told you that decision will largely shape the rest of your life? ☺

I was talking to our speaker at camp this week about his grown son. He told me how proud he was of his son and the family he was now raising. He said, "I can't imagine where he would be today if he had married one of the other girls he was serious about before he met his wife." His son and daughter-in-law are now a great example of a couple who are passionate about raising godly children and about ministering together as a couple.

As I thought about this, I was reminded of a gal you all know and love. When she was on our staff, she was engaged to a Christian man. The two of them came to us for some counseling before their marriage, which was a month away. As we talked to them about their dreams for the future, she shared her love for adventure, travel, and evangelism here and overseas. He was a computer nerd who loved the Lord and computers. He was satisfied to stay in one city the rest of his life, work 9–5, and raise a family. Both of them had reasonable dreams, but their two passions in life were very different. What was fulfilling for him was boring to her. What was exciting for her was terrifying to him.

At this stage in a relationship, many couples simply say, "it will work out" and, "we love each other." And many couples marry and live lives where one person never does that which he or she loves. Or, they *both* compromise, and miss out on living life putting their gifts and passions to the highest and best uses. We can all adapt, and there are plenty of times we do that out of love for our spouses. But why knowingly enter a relationship when you are passionate about very different things? (I am not talking about different vocations, but different passions.)

How do you recognize a difference in passions with a guy *before* you tie the knot?

I'm glad you asked! Before you met each other, what was he passionate about? Did he love ministry? Was he excited about serving others? Did he love adventure? Did you hear stories about him sharing his faith?

One summer, when one of you was involved in a romantic relationship with someone who was not at camp, you came to our cabin after a conversation with him on the phone. You told us he was upset at you because you hadn't called him earlier—but it was difficult for you to call him because you were "with your kids." You said to us, "Doesn't he understand that that is what I love doing, and that that is why I am here?" As you talked to your mom and me, I could hear you starting to process whether or not he understood your passion for ministry. It had nothing to do with your care for him, but a lot to do with his encouragement of you.

> We so want for you to find men who appreciate your gifts and encourage you to put your talents to their highest and best uses.

I want you to marry a man who loves to see you grow in your giftedness and passions. He should celebrate your opportunities, even when they come at his expense.

You know I do not mean that you and your future husband should ignore each other to pursue individual passions. I am talking about the heart condition. Is his heart overjoyed to see you growing and expressing your gifts and abilities? I hope so.

There are few things in life that give me more joy than seeing your mom and you girls "doing your thing"—and doing it so well. Kari, remember when we asked you to come to our parenting class and answer any questions the class might have of you before your mom and I started our lesson for the night? You sat down one hour later and class was over! We never got to speak that evening, but we were so proud that you had done your job and done it well.

All three of you have amazing abilities to minister to others. All three of you are years ahead of where your mom and I were at your age. We so want for you to find men who appreciate your gifts and encourage you to put your talents to their highest and best uses.

Love, Dad

P. S. Oh, what about the guy and gal on staff at camp? They broke their engagement. (Her parents were not too happy with us!) Eventually, she met a man who supported her passions, and they got married. The computer nerd also married someone of like passions in life.

How Important Are Common Interests?

Dear Kari, Lisa, and Julie,

Well, you are all back in school. What a great vacation we had together! Thanks for calling last night, Lisa; I'm glad your flight home went so well. Kari, hard to believe you've already started your last semester in college. We are so proud of you. Jules, well, it's the three of us again. We love having you home and cherish these last months before you are all out of the home.

In an earlier letter, I wrote about being unequally yoked to a non-believer—or to someone who is at a different place than you in your Christian walk. Today, I want to address the subject that first got me thinking about the problem of being "unequally yoked": how important it is for you to share similar interests or hobbies with your spouse. As in other areas, this is not necessarily a relationship stopper—as a believer marrying a non-believer would be—but it certainly is an area to evaluate and take seriously.

The most frequently mentioned concept for marriage in scripture is *oneness*. "The two will become one... they are no longer two."[1] I believe that if the "two" are not doing things together, then it is difficult for them to "become one."

Let's take the example that started this whole discussion. One night when you were all here and we were entertaining some of your staff friends from camp, your friend John was describing his relationship with a girl who was an outdoors sort of person. She loved hiking, swimming, running, walking, climbing, etc. She was very active and fit. John loved all the same things and activities she did. This is why he said he was shocked to find out she had recently married a man who did not enjoy any of those outdoor activities. Now, I am certainly not suggesting we marry clones of ourselves. However, in the area of interests, it is helpful to be on the same page.

In this era of "modern relationships," many couples solve this problem by having separate vacations or separate friends that share their interests. So the outdoor wife goes rock climbing with her friends for the weekend, and her indoor husband stays home with his drama-loving friends and takes in a few shows during the weekend. This seems to me to go against the "they are no longer two" concept. Again, I am not saying a couple should never separate for a weekend to do something one is passionate about and the other is not. What I *am* saying is that this should not be a pattern. It can be dangerous to spend increasing amounts of time with people of the opposite sex who have passions similar to one's own. A married woman might easily find herself especially enjoying time with a guy who also loves the outdoors. Or a married man may find that having cappuccino with his theater friends is much more rewarding than listening to his rock-climber wife talk about the great outdoors. Too often in these situations one will decide that the climbing partner or coffee drinker is really much more of a soul mate than the spouse.

Remember how John shared that his old friend, now a new bride, had called him to see if he wanted to go hiking for a few days since her new husband was not interested? John was very wise to decline her invitation—and she was foolish to have extended it. There is real danger here.

Are you able to know these things before marriage? You bet. I am always somewhat amused by the "couch potato" who joins the gym after "falling in love" with Mr./Miss Fitness. If it has not been a passion in the past, it will likely not be a passion in the future. In this area as in so many others, you will do much better to look at a man's history than to listen to his intentions for the future. Intentions keep us going only so long—and then we usually fall back into our regular patterns.

Sometimes this area of common interests is seen in what people are willing to "give up" for the relationship. In these cases they are not "taking up" that which they don't really like to please the other; they are giving up things they like to keep the other. I recall a woman who loved animals. She had a dog she adored. But because her fiancé didn't like animals, she got rid of the dog before they were married. The issue, of course, is not whether a couple should have a dog, or whether there are times when we are called to sacrifice something we love for the sake of the relationship. Rather, the issue is that if one person has a passion for animals and the other doesn't, it could become a continuing area of friction for the couple.

Your mom and I enjoy many of the same things. We have differing degrees of passion within our interests, yet we still are very similar. She loves the outdoors. I knew this not because I asked her if she would be willing to go camping after we got married, but because I knew she grew up camping and loved it. She also saw that I loved the outdoors and grew up camping as well. We both love to travel, to try new things, and to save money on trips!

Imagine that your boss comes in and announces that because the company has had such a great year, all the employees are being given a week off with full pay and $1,000 bonus money. Where would you go? What would you do? Who would you want to accompany you? Would your spouse be the one who came to mind to share these days and activities with?

Can you stay married to someone whose interests are opposite to yours? God calls us to do so if we are already married. Should you marry someone with interests opposite to yours? I would think twice on that one. It is so much easier to stay one with someone if you are walking in the same direction.

Love, Dad

Who Are
Your Counselors?

Dear Kari, Lisa, and Julie,

It has been great to have you responding to my letters with additional questions. Julie asked a question about how much one should listen to others regarding one's own relationships. I know that comes out of the context of having opinionated sisters, not to mention a mother and father who are willing to weigh in with observations about male suitors in her life!

Scripture says that in a multitude of counselors there is wisdom.[1] I think the key is knowing which of the multitude are giving wise counsel. How do you deal with conflicting counsel from people you respect?

When your mother and I were going together, I remarked to a mentor of mine that I couldn't understand why I wasn't physically attracted to Virginia. I told him how much I loved being with her, how much fun she was, how much I respected her personal walk with God, and how much I appreciated the way she served others—*but* I didn't feel physically attracted. His response was, "Go ahead and marry her. The physical attraction will come later." As much as I respected this man, I was not willing to take a chance on hoping that physical attraction would come. I had remained celibate for 25 years, and I was not about to marry someone whom I *hoped* I would grow to like physically.

Obviously, later the physical attraction came—but that's a letter for another time. Back to the multitude of counselors: what do you do with conflicting advice?

First, let me say that listening to counsel is a good thing. If you cut yourself off from those who might question your relationship because you don't want to hear anything that might "mess up a good thing," you are in trouble. People who are on the outside looking in usually are more objective about a relationship than we are.

Secondly, make sure that those you are listening to have the same biblical and moral standards that you do. Too many people have listened to those who don't share a common base for making their decisions. We will often ask someone if their advisors are solid, vital Christians. It could be you are involved with a "wonderful" man who shares everything with you except your faith. If your counselors are not people of faith, they will most likely not see this as an obstacle to marriage.

There are at least three scenarios regarding advice on relationships from others:

First is the case in which you like a young man very much and believe you are in love with him—but your family and friends don't think you are right together. Sometimes in these situations a typical response is, "You're all wrong. He is wonderful, he loves me, and I love him. You don't really know him, and after all, it is I who will be married to him, not you."

If you are the only one hearing God's affirmative response to a relationship, you might carefully consider whose voice you are really hearing. If your godly friends and/or family all have significant reservations, you should, at the very least, pause and examine the relationship more closely. A friend of ours has entered into marriage three different times, each time ignoring the cautions from family and friends. On the other hand, you should not call off a relationship simply because your family and friends are not all that excited about it. *You* are the only one walking down the aisle, making a *lifelong* commitment to another human being. We have counseled more than one woman who broke up with the man she loved because her family didn't approve, only to end up unhappily married to someone who may have been her family's first choice—but was her second choice. Ultimately, *you* must decide whom to marry. However, don't take lightly the sincere advice of those who know you best and love you most.

In the second scenario, there is someone you are not particularly attracted to, but you have been urged by others to continue in or pursue a relationship. Again, if these others are family members and friends who really know you and see something they feel you don't, it might be worth your while to listen. Do you remember the time a young man told your mom that he just didn't believe there were

> People on the outside looking in usually are more objective about a relationship than we are.

any godly, intelligent, fun, and beautiful women out there his age? Your mom (reminiscent of God's remark about Job), said, "Have you considered my niece, Rayna?"[2] While the decision about the relationship was certainly not up to your mom, the fellow was wise to seek the counsel of others. In situations like this where others see something you don't, it would be wise to pursue these discussions further with your friends and then pray and be open to God changing your heart. *But,* when you walk down the aisle, it must be because *you* are eager to spend the rest of your life with this man. It is not enough to walk down the aisle saying, "I really don't see that much in him, but my family and friends all think we are great together, so I guess I'll marry him." You wouldn't buy a car you don't like just because your friends like it, so why on earth would you consider marrying someone only a parent, sibling, or friend thinks is great? If your sister or friend thinks he's so great, let her marry him! God is big enough to bring together all the pieces of conviction, commitment, and chemistry.

The third scenario is the one where you are excited about a relationship and your family and friends confirm your desires. This, obviously, is the scenario you wish to aim for. This scenario is possible, given time, even when one of the first two scenarios is initially true. As I continue to say, "There is no rush on the second most important decision of your life." If you love him and others don't, wait. If others love him and you don't, wait. If you love him and others do as well, move ahead slowly and with caution. It is still the second most important decision you will ever make.

I want to end by saying that your mom and I are honored that you girls consider seriously our opinions about your male friends. Our prayer is that we will *all* clearly sense—with delight—God's best for each of you. Have I ever told you how hard it is for me to imagine anyone "good enough" for each of you? Good thing it's "what God has joined together,"[3] not "what Dad has joined together." Otherwise, you might never get married.

I love you—
Dad

Do You Like Him in Public?

Dear Kari, Lisa, and Julie,

You are all gifted "public" people. I love to watch you interact with individuals of all ages. You engage so well. I am so proud of how you carry yourself. I don't know what areas of ministry you will each end up in, but I suspect it will be in the public arena in some way.

I have seen it so many times: the painful look in a woman's eyes, so wanting her husband to be able to be engaging in public, as she is able to do. I want you to consider the fact that enjoying a relationship in private is one thing, while enjoying a relationship in the public arena is a different story.

I think Jim and Patty would be an example of this. Patty graduated second in her university class and was president of every organization she was ever involved in. She loved people and was at ease in any crowd. He, on the other hand, was very shy, was awkward in public, and wasn't self-motivated. When they were at public functions—even family gatherings—he would be off in the corner, disengaged. She was the life of the party, mingling easily, trying to "engage" him wherever she could. How could she have "fallen" for him?

She probably "fell" for him because he paid her attention,

adored her, and told her how wonderful she was. When they were alone, they had each other—and that was all that really mattered. She may have felt some twinge of "he's not that great at meeting my friends," but then most likely reasoned, "but most of our time we'll be alone anyway, and besides, I'm sure he'll change after a while."

He did change: he stopped being so wonderful when they were alone. Her constant involvement in public life and his awkwardness there left him feeling increasingly like a failure. Her "urging him on" became like a nagging mother to him. He started to withdraw and resent her.

Just last week, your mom and I were at a wedding reception dinner. As we sat down, I looked at my place setting and counted no less than eight pieces of silverware and three glasses. At Burger King I get one fork, one spoon, and one knife, along with a napkin, in a little plastic bag. But this! This was more than a little daunting.

Seriously, I felt out of my element. Fortunately for me, it was only one evening of mild discomfort. If I had married into a family that ate such meals on a regular basis, it would be different. Yes, I'm sure I could eventually learn the right order for using my utensils. However, this country boy would never fit permanently into high society.

Remember the movie *My Fair Lady*, in which the professor and his partner are determined to turn Liza Doolittle into a refined lady? My favorite part of that film is the scene at the horseracing track. After dutifully repeating all the phrases she has so carefully been taught, such as "How do you do?" and "The rain in Spain falls mainly in the plain," the race begins. The crowd around her is so elegant, so refined, so quiet. Finally, overcome by the slowness of "her" horse, she screams, "Move your blooming ass!" The crowd around her gasps, and the professor's mother faints. Liza Doolittle became again what she really was:

a street lady. There is nothing wrong with being a street lady—it was a valid culture of its own. But Liza simply did not fit into the professor's culture.

Bill and Carol had been married for thirty years when he told her he had never loved her. By God's mercy and their hard work, their marriage survived and grew. But Bill was a rough and tough cowboy, a gifted diesel mechanic, and Carol was a refined Dutch girl who loved craft shows and the "finer" things in life. She was attracted to this "wild" man who was cocky and fun. He was attracted to her incredibly refined beauty and grace. Not long after their marriage, neither was attracted to much in the other.

How can you detect this early on in a relationship? Perhaps you could consider these "tests": Are you happy, or are you terrified, when the two of you are invited to a family gathering or public event? Do you feel that you are constantly having to "drag him along"? Are you constantly called on to take the initiative in conversation in public? Does he "show well" with your friends? Would people say of the two of you, "They go together so well!" or rather, "Hard to explain love—I never would have put them together!"

I do not want any of you to marry your clone. How boring would that be! I do, however, want you to be married to someone you're proud to be with in public.

I sure am proud of each of you in public! You three are the best. I am most blessed to be your dad.

Love, Dad

Do You Like Being Alone Together?

Dear Kari, Lisa, and Julie,

In my last letter I asked, "Do you like him in public?" Today I want to ask the other question, "Do you like being alone with him?"

Over the years, we have met many couples who have been drawn to each other through their jobs or ministries. When they are working on a project together, they do great. Perhaps they lead a Bible study together and really enjoy partnering. As long as they have some common task to focus on, life is great. For many couples, raising children becomes the "task" they focus on, and that becomes the center of their universe. When they are alone they are talking about the children, working on projects for the children, vacationing with the children, etc.

After a talk at camp one summer, we gave couples a few questions and suggested they take the next half hour to share their feelings and perspectives on these areas of their life together. About ten minutes into the exercise, one wife came back into the main meeting room and asked us if we had seen her husband. We looked around at the coffee table, in the bathroom, and in all the "logical" places—to no avail. He was finally located in his child's classroom, scrunched down in the darkened corner as the class watched a video. When asked why he was there, he said, "I wanted to make sure what you were showing my child was acceptable." Right! He was just avoiding being alone with his wife.

Most couples would say that being alone during the courtship part of their relationship is no problem at all. For many of these couples it is because physical involvement has become a major part of their time together alone.

Other couples consider as "alone time" their time spent with other friends. This is a great way to enjoy each other, but it may not give you much insight into how your date is when alone with you. I've heard you girls talk about guys that are OK to be with in a group—there they follow the lead of others well, but get them alone and it's like pulling teeth to get a conversation going.

Some couples spend their alone time doing really outrageous stuff. They are always "going"—going to amusement parks, concerts, movies, baseball games, and more. It is always something that entertains you.

I am certainly not against all the above-mentioned activities, with the exception of premature physical involvement, but how do you do together when it is just the two of you? The two of you with no TV, no radio, and no other distractions? Do you enjoy just hanging out and talking? Does he enter your world and ask about things important to you? Does he connect emotionally with you? Do you find yourselves talking about any of the significant issues of life, or is it all "fluff?" Is there a spiritual dimension to your alone times? I'm not talking about prayer and Bible study, but rather whether the Lord is a meaningful part of your casual time together.

Now let me say that thankfully this is not a choose-A-or-B sort of question. Would you prefer (a) someone you were proud of in public but bored by in private, or (b) someone you loved being alone with but were embarrassed to be with in public? The correct answer would be: (c) someone you can be proud of in public and enjoy in private as well.

I was driving Julie to school the other day and she was asking about a theological issue; Lisa has been talking to us about her heart to reach her dorm wing for Christ; Kari has been asking for prayer for the women's conference she is speaking at. All three of you have "private hearts" that are deep, and public gifts that connect with others in a beautiful way.

My desire is for each of you to find a man whom you enjoy in public as well as in private, who also has a deep heart for Christ.

I love you each more than you know. I can hardly wait for us to be ministering together in Trinidad in two weeks. (I won't mind getting away from below-zero temperatures, either.)

Love, Dad

Chemistry

Marital Chemistry 101

Dear Kari, Lisa, and Julie,

I was blessed to have been raised in a strong Christian home. Your Grandpa Friesen always taught us that Christian character was to be demonstrated in all situations. He also taught us that godliness was the most important characteristic of a future mate. He would talk about how physical beauty was fleeting, but a woman of God was to be valued above all else. I agree with him to this day. What he never actually said, but what I extrapolated, was that it was impossible to be both physically beautiful and godly.

I grew up knowing that godliness was the most important trait in a mate, yet when I was honest I had to admit I wanted to marry a woman who was physically attractive to me. For some reason I was afraid that God would make me marry a woman who was "godly, but ugly." This fear demonstrated my inaccurate view of our loving Heavenly Father who longs to give all good things to His children. I am glad to say my view of God today is not of One who wants to withhold good gifts from His children, but of One who loves to lavish His children with good gifts.

I don't know whether my theology affected my experience or my experience affected my theology, but in your mom I found physical beauty and godliness all wrapped up in one person. The most incredible thing to me is that God in His goodness gave this godly beauty to *me*, one who is neither particularly handsome nor godly.

The three of you clearly defy my early view of God. You are each incredibly beautiful inside *and* out.

This is all by way of introduction to say that as you move toward marriage, be assured that God is fully capable of introducing you to someone who makes your heart both skip a beat and beat more strongly for the Lord at the same time. This certainly is not to say you are all to marry Mr. Universe—however, he should be Mr. Universe to you.

> Wait until you are able to walk down the aisle *confidently*, knowing that you are with the absolute best that "God has brought together."

Though chemistry is not what marriages should be based on, without chemistry there is little more than a nice roommate arrangement. As you read through the Song of Solomon, one cannot miss the passion for one another expressed by the two young adults.

I hate it when someone says flatly, "He's no Don Juan, but at least he will be a good provider," or, "At my age, I'm just glad I got *someone* to marry." I remember a wedding where the bride and groom hardly touched each other during the rehearsal or rehearsal dinner. They were polite to each other, but I certainly didn't see much spark. After the wedding ceremony, the couple stayed at the reception until everyone was gone, almost seeming to say, "Do we *have* to leave?" I want you to be so attracted to your fiancés that you must battle your desire to express your affection prematurely. I hope you bolt the reception as soon as it is "politely appropriate." The Lord surely designed us to have "chemistry."

Now—as your Grandpa Friesen said—"Godliness is essential." But don't forget that God is fully capable of giving you a husband who is best for you in *every* respect.

There are too many couples who walk down the aisle together because someone said, "You are perfect together!" There are too many couples who walk down the aisle with nagging doubts about their fiancés. Wait until you are able to walk down the aisle *confidently*, knowing that you are with the absolute best that "God has brought together."

I can see first-hand that it is possible to be a godly woman and a knock-out physically: I am living with four beautiful women who clearly demonstrate this truth. I am still working on believing that God has three godly, handsome men out there who are good enough for you... but my faith is still growing.

I am sure glad you look like your mom!

Love, Dad

Male/Female Differences and Sexuality

Dear Kari, Lisa, and Julie,

Yesterday, Annika Sorenstam created quite a furor as she became the first woman to play in the all-male PGA golf tournament in some forty years. We are living at a time when many are going to great lengths to demonstrate that there really are no differences between the males and females of our species—other than a few obvious physiological ones. The point of this letter, however, is not to comment on the PGA nor on the women's issue, but to talk to you about some of the differences between males and females in the area of relationship.

In the beginning, God created Adam and Eve—not Adam and Steve. From the very start of time, God determined that Adam needed a "helper" who was suitable to him, or literally: "like/opposite" him.[1] Before Eve was created, Adam had perfect communion with God, perfect communion with nature, and perfect communion with the animals. Furthermore, he lived in a perfect Garden. And yet, God said, "It is not good for the man to be alone." This was the *only* "not good" of creation. God demonstrated that we were created to live in community—we *need* each other. For most people, this need will be met in a mate. For those who are single, it is met by others in the Christian community.

Also note that God did *not* create Eve to be a maid to Adam, a slave who would pick up his clothes (he had none at the time, after all) or a cleaning woman who would mop up his messes. In no way was Eve created as an inferior creation. If anything, God was saying, "The man needs *help*." In fact, the word *helper* is often used in the Old Testament to refer to God himself.[2]

With that said, let me get back to the main focus of this letter. God created us *different*, as male and female, and it is important to understand this if we are to understand each other in the context of relationship.

Let's look first at how men and women view sex and relationship. When someone mentions the phrase "sexual relationship," most men think "sexual"—and most women think "relationship." This difference in perspective was God's idea.

God created men to be sexually stimulated visually and to be sexually aroused quickly; thus they think about sex frequently. Women, on the other hand, are not usually sexually stimulated visually, are physiologically aroused more slowly, and seldom think about sex.

Some women believe that because they are not tempted to stare at men walking down the street, or because they are not quickly aroused, or because they seldom think about sex, that they are therefore more "holy" than men. That may be true in some cases, but it has much more to do with the difference in our God-given wiring than with any difference in our morality.

To see how even our culture acknowledges this difference in wiring, consider how saturated society is with sexually explicit material designed for men, while very little is targeted for women. Men do *not* buy those magazines to "read the articles," no matter what they say. Let me quickly add that this barrage of visual stimulation is *never* an excuse for men to be involved in sexual sin. I'm simply observing that a society saturated with sexual imagery causes men to be constantly bombarded with temptation, and that such images tempt men far more than they tempt women.

Men generally are able to detach the sexual act from relationship; for most women, relationship is essential to the sexual act. Let me illustrate how this happens in marriage: a husband and wife have been bickering all afternoon long, with the feud continuing late into the evening. By 11 PM, they are barely speaking to each other. The husband rolls over in bed and says, "Want to 'do it?' " The wife says, "Do what?" The husband replies, "Have sex." The wife states, "But I don't even *like* you." To which the husband says, "So?" For women, relationship is the gateway to meaningful sex, while for men, sex is the gateway into meaningful relationship.

What does that have to do with you? When you're out with a man, he may act "relational"—taking you to dinner, talking, and bringing you flowers—fully expecting that the "payoff" will be sexual involvement at the end of the evening. Many women, on the other hand, will allow themselves to become physically involved with a man in order to keep him involved "relationally."

Just yesterday, your mom and I met with a woman who told us that she and her husband had done "everything" except actual intercourse before they were married. She went on to say that after they were married, her husband was frustrated when she refused to be involved in some of the same sexual acts she had agreed to prior to marriage. When we asked her why she refused, she said, "I don't have to do those things to keep him anymore—he's now my husband."

We have counseled countless couples who became involved sexually before marriage and are still dealing with the negative ramifications of it 10, 20, or even 30 years later. In fact, one couple I know have been married thirty years and have struggled for most of their marriage. They are both quite insecure in their love. She asks him, "How do I know you love me? Didn't you marry me only because I became pregnant?" He responds, "How do you think I feel, knowing these last thirty years that your parents resent that I 'made' you marry me because you were pregnant?"

I don't want to paint all men in a bad light, but let me be very clear on this: dating a man who says he wants to prove his love by becoming physically involved with you is like having dinner with a man who says he will show you how much he loves you by eating your serving of prime rib.

Most men, apart from the law of God, would be willing to have sex with most women. Sexual involvement is no demonstration of genuine love. Men do not frequent prostitutes to have a "meaningful relationship."

Many women run into major problems because they do not understand this concept. Because a woman's physical response is connected to relational commitment, she tends to assume that if her date desires deeper physical involvement, he is truly committed to her at a deep level relationally. Not necessarily true!

One of the ways you can know a man's love for you is by his desire to honor you and your relationship together by *not* becoming physically involved prematurely.

That's enough for today. Later on, I will write very specifically about just what constitutes premature physical involvement.

Thanks for making good choices in men. Not *all* men are beasts! ☺

Love you, Dad

You Asked
about Modesty

Dear Kari, Lisa, and Julie,

This afternoon Kari called and asked me a question about modesty. I reflected on the letters I have written you, and I am not sure that I have yet specifically dealt with that subject.

I remember when we were all on a family panel and someone asked about standards for modesty in our home. Julie answered that although your mom had opinions on this, my comments were especially thought-provoking. As I recall, Julie said that it had been helpful for me to describe what a man thinks when you dress immodestly. She said after I had given her a male perspective on how men view immodestly dressed women, she found it "disturbing and disgusting."

Defining modesty has always been a tricky thing. When I was a young man, the definition of modesty was quite different than today. I can remember hearing people say, "In some countries women *always* go topless and that's not seen as immodest, so why are we so uptight when someone shows a little cleavage?"

The principle given in 1 Peter 3:3 is that our "outward" appearance should not rob someone from seeing your inner beauty.[1] This means you should not dress so immodestly that someone notices only your body, but neither should you cover yourself up so much that attention is drawn to the odd way you dress.

Though the definition of modesty may vary by culture, it is usually determined by how men respond to the dress of the women. Notice that scripture does not address the issue of dress for men—just for women.

Because we are wired so differently as men and women, it may be helpful for me to give you a glimpse into a man's mind as he observes women. My being quite blunt is not meant to be inappropriate, but to be honest, so you have a better understanding of the mind of a man.

When you wear something where your breasts are partially exposed, it is sexually exciting to men. Scripture talks openly about the sexual satisfaction that a wife's breasts bring in the marriage relationship. Proverbs 5:19 says, ". . . Let her [your wife's] breasts satisfy you at all times..." Exposure of the breast is sexually stimulating. Since the only breasts that are meant to sexually stimulate a man are the breasts of his wife, why would a Christian woman knowingly dress in a way that exposes her breasts to men other than her husband?

When a man sees a woman in a tight-fitting top, he usually attempts to figure out if she has a bra on or not. If she has only spaghetti straps, this adds to the intrigue. Tops that are so tight or sheer in nature that he is able to see a woman's nipples are especially stimulating.

Another area of sexual interest for men is the genital area. When women pour themselves into pants so that every curve and indentation is noticeable, it becomes a focal point and is sexually exciting.

Legs have also been a focal point for men. High skirts or short shorts simply tend to draw men's eyes to "more flesh."

In general, the more flesh exposed, the more temptation there is for men. It may sound odd, but a fairly simple test is to see how men tend to look at you. If strangers follow you with their eyes, it is generally not a good thing.

Your mom was exemplary in this area. My memory of her is that she usually dressed in jeans and a loose-fitting button-up blouse. It wasn't until after we were married that I realized how incredibly beautiful her whole body was—if you know what I mean.

You three girls are all physically beautiful. But if you flaunt your physical beauty, you are in essence saying you believe *that* is the best part of you. The truth is, your inner beauty is breathtaking. Don't dress in a way that men miss seeing your inner beauty—or you may miss a man who is drawn to the beauty of your whole being.

I love you —
Dad

Only Big Lures Catch Prize "Fish"

Dear Kari, Lisa, and Julie,

As you know, I'm not much of a fisherman, but I do know that you catch certain types of fish with certain types of lures. If you want to catch a marlin, you use a very large lure that looks like a fish. Smaller fish will not even attempt to bite the lure because it is "out of their class" in size. Fishermen who use such lures are limiting themselves to a select type of fish. Those who use a smaller lure are much more apt to catch a variety of fish that would bite at the smaller lure. So, you might ask, if a smaller lure attracts more fish, why would anyone use a large lure that would "self-select" a much rarer and distinct type of fish? The answer is that you use the large lure specifically because you *want* to catch a rarer and distinct type of fish.

I am not suggesting that you go "fishing" for a husband or try to land "a big one." But I do want to offer some principles that will help you to "self-select" a distinct type of man.

Today, your mom and I met with your cousin Stephanie and her husband Steve, who have now been married two and a half years. As we talked, I asked them to tell me again a bit about their dating and courtship. I knew they had been careful in their physical expression, so I asked them just how they had arrived at their standards for physical expression in dating. Steve replied that he had always had a conservative standard, but it was Stephanie who stated she did not want to kiss a man until they were engaged. Now *that* is a "big lure." That is a huge self-selecting lure. Most men would not even be interested in such a challenge. They are much too "small."

> The goal is not to find a date, but to find a godly man.

Steve is a "stud." But he was interested in a woman of such standards, so for the next six years he and Stephanie dated without kissing. In my book, he is a "real man" because he waited to marry a "real woman" and did not settle for a woman who would compromise her standards. A woman who sets such a standard may not have as many dates as her girlfriends who are using "smaller lures." If you are willing to get physically involved with a guy early in the relationship, you normally will have no problem in finding a date. The goal, however, is not to find a date, but to find a godly man.

The way a woman dresses is also a "lure" used to catch a man. Since men are visually stimulated and attracted by the opposite sex, a woman is able to gain more attention the less modestly she is willing to dress. But, again, what kind of guy do you want to attract? The problem created by attracting a man with your body is you need to "keep him" with your body. However, the reality is that women age—there will always be women with better bodies than yours, and, unfortunately, plenty of them won't mind that your husband is a married man.

The other sobering reality is that if a man is attracted to you because of your body, he will most likely be checking out other bodies all the time.

You have been at summer camps long enough to observe how campers tend to "find their level." The gals who arrive that first day advertising their bodies will soon be surrounded by guys who are interested in staring at them or trying out the "merchandise."

I am always sadly amused when girls come up to your mom and me and express how upset they are with the guys they are going out with. "They are all losers," one will say. "All they want is to get their hands all over me!" "*Really?*" I say, as I try to look aside so as not to sin by staring at her form-fitting, low-cut tank top. She is getting exactly the type of guy who is attracted to the cheap "little" lures.

As you know, your mom has always been a conservative dresser. I remember that when we were getting to know each other, she would usually wear loose-fitting button-down shirts. She was and still is beautiful, there is no doubt about that. But she always dressed—and still does—in a way that you would be struck by and attracted to her character, not her body. 1 Peter 3 instructs women to dress modestly so that others can see their "inner" beauty.[1]

I will never forget our wedding night, when I saw her naked for the first time. Wow—she was a knockout! I knew she was beautiful, but she had dressed in a way that I never knew *how* physically beautiful she was.

Well, what is the point of this fish story? Simply this: in all our years of living on Catalina Island, no one ever ran to the pier to watch someone bring in a ten-inch mackerel. The cannon was never shot off to announce that a twelve-inch bonita had been caught. No one ever mounted a three-inch anchovy over his mantel.

The fish that were mounted, or had the cannon shot off to herald their arrival, or had people oohing and ahhing on the pier, were the very rare, distinct fish. May God continue to help you to fish only with the "big" lures of modesty, purity, and godliness.

I promise you, if you bring home such a rare catch, I won't kill him and mount him over our fireplace! But I *will* proudly say, "Look at that rare find. He is distinct. I am so thankful my daughter didn't settle for any ol' fish, but fished with a lure that attracted only the best."

You are rare and distinctly beautiful ladies; don't ever settle for some little ol' mackerel.

Where You "Fish" Does Affect Your "Catch"

Dear Kari, Lisa, and Julie,

It is *so* good having you all home for Christmas. I love seeing you interact together. God has done some wonderful things in your lives. It's fun to just "hang out" with you. Thanks for continuing to let us into your lives.

I want to follow up on the letter I wrote a few months ago regarding lures. If you remember, I said that the type of "lures" you use will greatly determine what kinds of "fish" are attracted to you. I stated that if you use a "little" lure such as dressing immodestly or being sexually permissive, you could always attract a man, but he was unlikely to be a "prize fish." On the other hand, using a "big" lure such as modesty and sexual purity would attract mainly "prize fish."

As I thought about this illustration, it struck me that it is possible to fish with the right kind of lure, but in the wrong place. This will, most likely, not land you a prize fish either. For instance, you might use the best "big" lure there is, but if you troll in shallow water close to the shore, you will never catch a "prize fish," such as a marlin or swordfish, because marlins and swordfish simply don't swim in shallow water. When fishing for game fish, you need to fish in deeper waters.

Often, on the marine radio, you will hear the captain of a fishing vessel broadcasting to his friends, telling them in what area the marlin or swordfish are running. Pretty soon a number of boats will converge on an area where the game fish have been spotted.

Now, how does this translate into making the second most important decision of your life?

Simply this: if you spend your free time on weekends hanging out at clubs, bars, or frat parties, you are less likely to find the sort of guy who will have the values that make a great husband. Girls will make statements like, "I just can't find any Christian guys." One simple question would be, "Are you frequenting the spots where Christian guys tend to be, or are you 'hanging too close to shore?'"

Let me add, however, that just because a guy hangs out at church doesn't make him a strong Christian, any more than hanging out at McDonald's makes you a hamburger. To return to the fish analogy, "little fish" do sometimes swim in deep waters; but seldom do "big fish" swim in shallow waters.

As I was writing this, a woman came by and asked what I was doing. I told her about the letter I was writing. She is recently divorced from a "small fish" who swam in deep waters. She said, "Make sure you say that not all fish who swim in deep waters are keepers."

I trust that many of the letters I am writing will help you to be selective about all men. However, you can save yourself a lot of grief simply by not fishing in the wrong areas, as well as by using the correct lure for the type of fish you wish to catch.

I may be getting into water over my head, but I want to keep the analogy going just a bit further: after hooking the prize fish, you may bring it up alongside the boat and decide it is not a "keeper." It may be too small or diseased, or perhaps you realize you're not ready to "land one" yet, so you "tag and release."

But if you don't fish in the right area you will never have the opportunity to examine the catch more closely.

My regret for many a woman is that she hooks up with a small fish, caught in the wrong area, and, never having hooked up with a prize fish, simply settles for whatever "slimy thing" she has landed. She says, "He looks, smells, and seems like a fish—and this late in the day, who knows if I'll ever hook another one?" Therefore, she keeps the fish, only to find out later that it really isn't that tasty. Perhaps it would have been worth the effort to go out into deeper water after all.

Girls, I am so thankful you have—for the most part—fished in deep waters. Don't get discouraged if there don't seem to be many "fish in the sea." In relationships as in fishing, patience is a great virtue. No fish is far better than the wrong fish, and no man is far better than the wrong man.

May God continue to help you set your standards high and to fish accordingly.

Love, Dad

Take a Look
Before Taking the Hook

Dear Kari, Lisa, and Julie,

I promise this will be my last "fishing" letter, but talking to the woman who suggested we warn you that not all "fish" who swim in deep waters are keepers, caused me to take a look at this from the "prize fish" point of view.

I know without any doubt that you each are "prize fish." So, the question would be: If you are the prize fish swimming in deep waters, how do you make sure you are swallowing a "real mackerel" and not a fancy fake lure?

My understanding is that a game fish will sometimes "hit" on a lure because it "looks" real, but it will first carefully play with the lure in its mouth, realize it is not real, and spit it out. The danger with swallowing *without* examining is that by the time you realize the bait was fake, you are hooked!

Now, it doesn't take a rocket scientist to figure the point of this illustration. I'm thinking here of many women we have counseled: each was swimming in the right waters and met a guy who seemed to be wonderful. He looked like a mackerel and appeared to swim like a mackerel. Because she was so eager to have a mackerel, she bit—and swallowed hard. She was hooked.

Once she realized she had swallowed a fake lure, it was too late. The hook was deep inside her and she was not able to free herself. Perhaps she was never instructed on how to detect fake lures. I will admit that the "Deceiver Lure Company" makes some mighty *real* looking lures! Which is why—before you swallow that lure—you need to "play" with it to see if it is real.

Let me take a shot at some of the ways women may swallow too quickly and get hooked on a "fake" lure.

Some women bite quickly, afraid that if they don't, the mackerel will get away and they will "never have another chance to catch a fish."

Some women simply look at his appearance and get excited about this guy that looks so "hot." Many women see the outward appearance and make a lot of assumptions about the character that "must" go with those blue eyes.

Many women are so desirous of a relationship that they are in love with love rather than with a specific man. These women so want to be loved that they tend to be blind to the character flaws in a man and see only the romantic relationship they had always dreamed of. Later they realize that they married figments of their imaginations and that their dreams have become nightmares.

Some women get physically involved too soon and lose all objectivity in the relationship. Some marry a man they have become too physically involved with believing it will make their sin "right." Some feel that they must marry a man because he was the first man she had sex with and so the "right thing to do" is to marry the man. Some marry men they have been physically involved with just so they will never have to admit to this sin. Whatever the reason, premature physical involvement is a huge hook that, when swallowed too quickly, often hooks deeply.

So how do you know the real mackerel? The bottom line is: *don't swallow too quickly.*

Do you remember how your mom would save spoiled milk

without labeling it so she could cook with it at a later time? (You know her stewardship heart would not allow her to throw anything away.) Well, she knew what container held spoiled milk and, for some reason, she assumed we would know as well. Lisa, it seems, was the one caught by this most often. She loved milk, and would often pour a big glass and gulp away, only to gag on it as she realized—a quarter of a glass too late—that the milk was spoiled!

> The sad reality is that, at first look, things—and people—are not always what they appear to be.

So, how can you *really know* what a man is like? Spend time with him in every possible setting. Remember the "Four Seasons Rule." Hang out with his family, observe him in social situations, watch him when he has failed, and take note of him when he is tired or sick. In other words, take your time to check the "bait" to see if it is truly the real thing. The sad reality is that, at first look, things—and people—are not always what they appear to be.

The principle to be aware of is the concept of wolves in sheep's clothing. You girls will always have men that will want to be with you. One of your greatest challenges will be to discern the real character of the men you meet and not get involved with them physically, socially, emotionally, or spiritually without examining them carefully before getting "hooked."

It is a real gift to have a friend who is able and willing to objectively make observations about "bait" you may be tempted to swallow too quickly. Just today, your mom was talking to me about a woman she is counseling. A man is pursuing her and she is tempted to reciprocate. But your mom believes this man is an impostor who has learned enough "Christian lingo" to impress the woman, while his character raises significant questions regarding the sincerity of his faith. Your mom is able to see this much more clearly than the woman, who has let herself get hooked prematurely.

Well, that's enough about fishing.

Love, Dad

What Does God Think about Sex?

Dear Kari, Lisa, and Julie,

Before I start writing about physical relationships, I thought it might be good to write about what God thinks about sex in the first place. Much of this will be "review" for you, but I will feel better having it put in writing.

God loves sex. He created it. He made it pleasurable. He designed it to be expressed only within the safety of marriage.

Many times, we Christians are almost apologetic about sexuality, as though it were something we're embarrassed or ashamed about. "Oh, I don't do sex—I'm a Christian." Christians, of all people, should be *positive* about sexuality. Our Heavenly Father created it. Satan had no part in its creation. (Though you can be assured that if God created something beautiful for pleasure, Satan will attempt to turn it into misery and heartache.)

God could have accomplished reproduction any way He wanted. He could have designed us to become pregnant when we pick our noses. However, He decided to make this sex thing not only functional, but pleasurable, as well. He has made us, physiologically, in such a way that married couples are able to enjoy sexual intimacy whether or not it results in pregnancy.

Often, when Christians think of sex, the first word that comes to their minds is "don't." Some even feel that there is something *wrong* with sex, or that it is something we should not talk about. I believe, however, that the words for us regarding sex before marriage should not be "bad, don't"—but "great, wait."

To the embarrassment of some, I actually performed an original rap emphasizing this truth at a recent True Love Waits—Family Edition we sponsored.

> *Sex is great; it's worth the wait,*
> *But Satan tries to imitate*
> *By getting you to fornicate.*
> *Naked was God's designed state*
> *For married couples to celebrate.*
> *Sex is great; it's worth the wait,*
> *So wait for God's chosen mate.*

God's Word is very specific and explicit about the delights of sexual expression. The passage in scripture that your mom says I know the best is Proverbs 5:18–19 (NASB): ". . . rejoice in the wife of your youth. . . . let her breasts satisfy you at all times; be exhilarated always with her love." These verses talk about the delight of a sexual relationship with your wife. It is erotic, exciting, satisfying—and *exclusively* expressed with the wife of your youth.

God has given us our sexuality as a gift. If He didn't want us to enjoy it, He wouldn't have created it. If He didn't love us so much, He wouldn't have given us such clear directives regarding how we are to express our sexuality. I trust, in the letters to follow, you will be increasingly convinced how much God loves you and desires to give you His best in this area as in every other area of life.

Scripture says how sexual sin is different from all others.[1] I believe that is because sex is such a special gift from God to married couples. May God continue to keep you convinced of how good it is to follow Him fully in all areas of life.

Love, Dad

Don't Awaken Love Until Its Time

Dear Kari, Lisa, and Julie,

Last weekend, we sponsored a True Love Waits—Family Edition conference at the church. Lisa and Kari, you would have been proud of Julie, she presented so well. Your mom and I sure were proud of her.

You have heard us speak on relationships many times, but this weekend I used a new illustration, and I want to share it with you.

I asked for a volunteer and brought up a high school girl who had mentioned earlier that evening that she dated a lot. I asked her to close her eyes and identify the fruit I gave her to taste. Earlier that afternoon I had gone to the grocery store and asked the produce man for the greenest bunch of bananas he had. He gave me a bunch that was pure green. I peeled one of these bananas and gave the volunteer a bite. She spit it out—and accused me of giving her the peel! I then asked her to open her eyes, and she saw that she had in fact bitten down on a banana. I asked, "What's wrong?" and she said, "It wasn't ripe!" I then gave her a bunch of beautifully ripe bananas.

The reason I used this illustration is that I was teaching out of the Song of Solomon where the same exact phrase is used three times: "Do not stir up or awaken love until the appropriate time." (HCSB).[1] So often, in discussions around physical expression prior to marriage, the impression is that God is in some way against sex. You may hear someone say, "If God is so in favor of sex, why did He put on all these restrictions as to when it can be expressed?" Remember the banana: God created bananas for us to enjoy! As *The Message* version of those verses in the Song of Solomon says, "Don't excite love, don't stir it up, until the time is ripe—and you're ready."

I know this analogy is a stretch for you, since none of the three of you like bananas. Many people, however, do enjoy a nice, ripe banana. When shopping for fruit, they will pass over the green bananas and select a bunch that is yellow and ready to eat.

The truth is not that God doesn't want us to enjoy sex; it is that He wants us to enjoy it *in its fullness*. He clearly states that we are not to taste it until it is ripe.

Unfortunately, your mother and I have met with many couples who "tasted the fruit before its time" and then struggled after getting married to enjoy physical intimacy—they got a bad taste in their mouths early on because their initial intimacy wasn't expressed within the safety, security, and covenant of marriage.

Speaking as a male, I am sorry to say that many men will say they think "green bananas" are *great*. After all, eating green bananas will help the bananas ripen... ri-i-ight! May I say that many men are not very discerning when it comes to fruit and women?

A man who sees your relationship as one that is "ripening," who wants to protect it so that someday you and he can enjoy it in its fullness, is a mature man.

Mature men wait for the fruit of love to ripen. Immature men can't wait to taste the fruit and thus make it impossible for that fruit to ripen as it was designed to.

In subsequent letters I will write very specifically about setting physical boundaries, but for today I just want to again emphasize that the reason God says, "Do not stir up or awaken love until it is ready" is not that He is against us enjoying physical intimacy with our spouses. Because this intimacy is such a special gift, He wants to protect us from exposing it too soon.

Not to take this illustration *too* far, but as I am writing this it occurs to me that God put the peel on the banana to protect it until it is ripe. When the fruit is ripe, it is not only acceptable but also necessary to remove the peel to enjoy the fruit. If that protective peel is removed too soon, however, the banana will never ripen properly—it will simply rot.

The good news for those who have exposed the fruit prematurely is that we serve a God who forgives and is able to make something beautiful out of that which we mess up. Your mom loves to take rotten bananas and make banana bread. She redeems the bananas, if you will, and makes them into something wonderful and delicious. God is the "celestial baker" and is fully capable, after we repent, of making good out of our sinful choices. But it is not like eating a fresh, ripe banana. You have only one opportunity for that.

Well, that's enough for today. As we approach Thanksgiving, I want you each to know how very thankful I am for you and the choices you have made regarding "fruit."

May God continue to give you patience to let the fruit of His choice ripen for you in His time.

With my love, Dad

What Constitutes Sexual Purity?

Dear Kari, Lisa, and Julie,

Last night at camp, we showed the video *Sex Has a Price Tag* to the junior highers, high schoolers, and parents as an optional meeting.[1] One boy who was entering junior high asked his dad if he could see the video. His dad in turn asked him if he knew what sex was. The boy confidently answered, "Yes." So the son and his dad viewed the video. After the video, the boy looked up at his dad and asked, "What are genitals?" His father explained, and then proceeded to describe the process of conception. The boy looked shocked and exclaimed, "You and mom did that?!" I laughed when I heard it, but then thought how many youth say confidently, "Yeah, I know all about sex," when really they hardly have a clue.

I was thinking of the letter you received, Kari, from the girl who had heard your mom and me give a talk on sexuality. We know her parents are strong Christians, so we were a bit surprised to read her words:

> *I wish I had heard your parents talk about what sex*
> *was before I made so many mistakes.*

She was referring to the question we put forth to the high schoolers: "What does God say about sex?" Their resounding answer was "Don't do it until you are married!" We then asked, "What *is* sex?" The teens answered this question much less confidently. One student said, "Sex is getting pregnant." Another said sex was "going too far." After their numerous attempts at a definition, we suggested to them that sex is "anything that stimulates the body sexually." This would include what in marriage manuals is called "foreplay"—anything that excites and prepares the body for sexual intercourse.

Your mom and I have added a new part to our "banana" talk. We have always talked about the banana peel being God's protection to cover a banana while it matures so that it can be eaten and enjoyed when it is ripe. We try to help teens see that God's command to keep sex for marriage is like His putting the peel on a banana. It isn't because we *can't* eat green bananas—they aren't poisonous—but they are not ripe yet, as God designed them to be for our pleasure. Obviously, your mom and I have always stressed in our talks that you shouldn't "peel the banana" until you are married.

One day, as we were presenting the banana talk, it occurred to me that the highest goal for many Christian couples is getting to the altar without the "banana being peeled." Your mom and I were once counseling an engaged Christian couple, and before we had talked very long, the young woman said with confidence, "We are committed to not having sex before we are married." We affirmed them, and then asked what their level of physical involvement was. The woman's eyes turned downward as though the answer might be written on the floor. When she didn't speak, we gently asked, "Have you fondled each other?" "Yes," she answered. "Have you been naked together?" "Yes," she said. "Have you masturbated each other?" "Yes," she said again. She had been taking pride in the fact that they were technically virgins.

For many, the goal is getting to the altar with the peel still on the banana—yet they have fondled each other or engaged in "foreplay" of some kind. As I describe this while giving the banana talk, I now squeeze and pinch the banana—this is the new part. By the time I finish talking, though the banana has not been peeled, it's completely mush inside: not the way God designed bananas to be eaten. One time, while I was speaking and illustrating this point, I realized the banana peel had split open.

I explained to the students that the peel hadn't technically been peeled, but had "accidentally" been split. How similar this is to physical involvement! "We didn't *mean* to have sex... it just happened!" or "It was an accident!" I love what Pam Stenzel says in *Sex Has a Price Tag*: "The only way sex is an 'accident' is if you are

> Just as we are careful to protect fruit so it won't get bruised, we need to carefully protect our relationships.

walking naked down the street and someone else comes along walking toward you naked, and you accidentally collide."

All sex is intentional sex. There is no such thing as sex being an "accident." We make many choices that lead to physical involvement that may eventually culminate in sexual intercourse.

The question often asked is, "How far may I go?" In other words, we are asking, "How much can we play with the banana without having its peel crack?" The Pharisees were especially good at asking such questions.[2] In essence, we are asking, "How close to sin can we get?" But, just as we are careful to protect fruit so it won't get bruised, we need to carefully protect our relationships so we will not damage what God wishes to be fresh for marriage.

Someone once generously gave our family a subscription to Harry and David's "Fruit of the Month Club." Each month, we would receive a different box of delicious fruit. And each month, I was newly impressed with the very elaborate packaging included to ensure the fruit would be protected. If it is worth so much to protect mere fruit, how much more important is it for us to protect the gift of sex until marriage!

Well, that's enough for tonight. I'll write next about specific guidelines for physical involvement.

You girls are the best fruit I have ever seen. Make sure you take great efforts to protect yourself for God's best.

Love, Dad

Four Scriptural Guidelines for Physical Involvement

Dear Kari, Lisa, and Julie,

Well, how far is too far? This is the question most often asked by youth regarding physical involvement. It in itself is a telling question because in essence it is saying, "How close to sin can I get, without being guilty of sinning? (If the answer is that kissing for 12 seconds is not sin, but 13 seconds *is* sin, then give me your lips and a stopwatch and let's go at it!)" This is the sort of answer the Pharisees were always after. They were looking to accomplish the "letter of the law without the spirit of the law."[1] A much better question for a couple to ask—rather than "How far can I go?"—is "How honorable and pure can I be?"

I have heard many young people be taught that "sex before marriage is wrong—and you should pray about all the other stuff." I hate to question the power of prayer, but somehow I doubt its effectiveness when a couple is in the back seat of a car making out and praying, "Lord, please show us how far to go." Either the prayers are not heard or the response does not get through—because seldom have couples been helped by prayer in such situations.

God has given us His objective word to help us with guidelines for physical involvement prior to marriage. Remember,

God's guidelines for dating couples are the same as His guidelines for couples one day before their wedding. In God's eyes you are either married—or you are *not*.

Here are at least four scriptural guidelines for physical involvement prior to marriage.

1. No sexual intercourse before marriage—ever! (Matt. 19:5)[2]

Not "But he is going off to war and what if he gets killed and has never had sex?" or "We are planning on getting married as soon as our finances work out, so what's the big deal?" or "We really do love each other and feel this is just an extension of our spiritual and emotional lives." God is not saying "no sex before marriage" to make our lives miserable, but to save us from heartache. Matthew 19:5 describes the very clear process of becoming one flesh: first you leave home, becoming independent from your parents. Next, you cleave to your mate, making a lifelong commitment to him legally, usually through a marriage ceremony. Lastly, and only after the first two have been accomplished, you become one flesh. This is because after leaving home and cleaving to another for life, you have the security to establish a sexual relationship—knowing that your physical expression of love can continue to grow and develop for your whole life. Becoming one flesh is not a tryout; it is a permanent relationship. Just today I received an email from a dad in our church regarding his daughters. Let me share a couple of his sentences as an illustration of why God said to have sexual intercourse only after marriage.

Becoming one flesh is not a tryout; it's a permanent relationship.

> *I think you knew Sue opted for abortion despite the counseling and parental support to choose otherwise. Her boyfriend (the baby's father) broke up with her, which depressed her greatly.*
>
> *Our other daughter, Julie, announced her pregnancy and had an abortion practically before we could even respond. She also has broken up with her boyfriend.*

God so wants to spare all the heartache: both the couple's and the parents'—and, in these two cases, spare the lives of two unborn children as well.

2. *Do not be selfish with your love. (1 Corinthians 13:5)*[3]

True love is not selfish. It always wants what is best for the other person. It is not driven by selfish desires. For many men, the selfish desire is simply to have a biological appetite satisfied. It has little or nothing to do with love. As someone once said, "Lust can't wait to get, Love can't wait to give." I believe many women selfishly enter into physical relationships because they are desperate to have someone—and feel that sex will "keep" a relationship going.

If a guy tells you that he truly loves you and wants to prove it by being sexually active with you, what he really means is: "I have a sexual urge that I want to satisfy. I really don't care if you become pregnant, or contract a sexually transmitted disease that could kill you or leave you sterile for life. My urge is so strong that I am willing say anything to get you to have sex with me, even though it will likely cause significant emotional damage to you. Please remember—the reason I am doing this is because I love you." Hogwash—dump the pig.

3. *Treat each other in all purity. (1 Timothy 5:2)*[4]

To treat each other "purely" is to treat each other in a way that is without compromise. Webster defines "pure" as "free from anything that adulterates, taints, or impairs." Put another way, something is "pure" when it is "how it was designed to be." I think of something "pure" as something I am not ashamed of. In the physical arena, pure actions are those actions that I would not be ashamed of were I to be "walked in on."

A true story that illustrates this last definition took place between a Christian man and woman who were engaged to be married. They had not consummated their relationship physically, but decided they wanted to do so before their wedding night—in a romantic atmosphere. It happened that the man's parents were very wealthy and had an incredible house. One weekend, the parents were going away and asked their son if he would come and house-sit for the weekend. The engaged couple thought this would be the perfect time to consummate their relationship physically.

That evening, they put their plan into action. Then, after they were both naked, the phone rang. The young man's father was on the phone. He apologetically stated that he had left the computer on with some important programs running, and asked his son to go to the basement and turn it off. Being in a playful mood, the young man picked his naked fiancée up and carried her downstairs. As they opened the basement door, the lights came on and the whole church yelled, "Surprise!" His parents

> In over 25 years of counseling, *no one* has ever said to me they wished they had messed around more before they were married.

had arranged the whole thing to throw a surprise engagement party for the young couple.

Were the couple embarrassed? You bet! Were they ashamed? Absolutely! Now, imagine the same scenario, except that the couple descending into the basement is married and the church is throwing a surprise anniversary party. Would that couple be embarrassed? You bet! Would they be ashamed? Absolutely not. God delights in married couples being naked together; they have nothing to be ashamed of.

4. Do not lust after each other. (1 Thessalonians 4:3–8)[5]

The word "lust" simply means "a strong desire." When used in the context of sexual expression, it means to desire something that is not appropriate at the time. Since sexual intercourse is not appropriate until marriage, it would mean to be physically or mentally involved with someone in such a way that the mind is "having sex" even if the body isn't. Men are wired so they start to lust very easily. If a man says he can french kiss and fondle you and not be lusting, either he is a liar, or something is not quite "normal" with the man physiologically.

⌒

If you apply these four scriptural guidelines, your physical involvement with your date will be considerably less than that of many of your friends. I firmly believe that your heartache will be considerably less as well.

Have I told you yet that in over 25 years of counseling, *no one* has ever said to me they wished they had messed around more before they were married? Many, however, have said they wished they had remained pure.

May God give you joy in following the whole counsel of God—and may you find men who have also found such joy.

Love, Dad

Four Practical Guidelines for Physical Involvement

Dear Kari, Lisa, and Julie,

This morning, we met with a man who was talking with us about a very good friend of his: a woman who became pregnant by a man she no longer has any relationship with. The pregnant woman was raised in a Christian home and had had all the relationship teaching one could have. Your mom and I have talked a great deal about how those who know biblical principles so often desert them in their physical relationships.

The four guidelines Robbie Castleman presents in her book *True Love in a World of False Hope* are about the best practical guidelines we've come across for helping couples to honor God and each other in their physical relationships.[1]

The first guideline she gives is "Four on the floor." Your two feet and your boyfriend's two feet should remain on the floor at all times. This avoids compromising positions. It means, for example, if you are watching a movie together, you sit side by side on the couch instead of putting your head on his lap as you lie on the couch. It also keeps you from lying in bed together at any time. If you follow this guideline, you will significantly reduce the temptation to be physically involved.

The second guideline is "Hands off." This means you keep

you hands off what we have all been taught are "private parts." In order to reduce sexually stimulating one another, you refrain from fondling each other over or under your clothes. Any guy who says he can fondle a girl's breast without getting sexually stimulated is in the same camp with guys who say they read *Playboy* magazine for the articles.

The third guideline is "Clothes on." This means that you each have a commitment to keeping your clothes on at all times. You do not push them up, pull them down, unbutton, or unzip them. They stay fully on at all times when you are together. This also speaks to the issue of modesty. Since men are sexually stimulated visually, girls do a great service to their spiritual brothers by dressing in a way that does not attract attention to their bodies.

The fourth guideline is "Tongue in." This addresses the area of French kissing. You keep your tongue in your own mouth. The reason for this guideline is that French kissing is the beginning of foreplay, sexually arousing the body for the purpose of intercourse.

The purpose of these guidelines is to decrease temptation before marriage and to help you to honor each other sexually.

Some people we have talked to see these guidelines as "quaint" or old-fashioned. They insist that in today's enlightened times, such rules are really archaic.

It is true that not every couple who watch a movie with their feet off the floor end up compromising themselves physically. Some would argue you could fondle without sinning. (In my experience, men who fondle do sin, either by lusting or lying.) It is hard for me to imagine a couple not compromising God's design for relationships if they become naked together before marriage. Finally, not every couple who French kiss end up in bed together. *However*, couples who follow these four guidelines will be much less likely to compromise themselves and live with regrets in regard to their physical relationship.

I can say with certainty that the pregnant girl I referred to earlier did not follow these guidelines. You do not get pregnant if you keep four feet on the floor, keep your hands off each other's private parts, keep your clothes on, and keep your tongue in your own mouth.

You will have your whole life to enjoy your spouse sexually. Sex is a wonderful gift from God that many struggle to experience fully—because they did not protect it prior to marriage.

I am thankful that your mom and I were virgins when we were married. We did pretty well on the four principles; however, I can tell you that if we had known and followed these guidelines completely, they would have reduced some of the stress in our relationship.

Have I ever told you how much I love you and wish the very best for you in your relationships?

Love, Dad

The Fallacy of Parallel Physical Involvement

Dear Kari, Lisa, and Julie,

Over the years, as we have counseled many individuals and couples yet to be married, we have come across a widely accepted paradigm for physical relationships which I will call "parallel thinking."

Basically, "parallel thinking" says that all aspects of a relationship should grow in a parallel fashion prior to marriage. It contends that the emotional, spiritual, and physical aspects of a relationship should deepen in roughly an equally increasing manner. In other words, this "parallel" involvement would call for a limited physical expression early in a relationship (when there is little emotional and spiritual connection). But as the relationship grows in the areas of the emotional and spiritual, according to this school of thought, the physical involvement should follow suit.

We often ask couples how they will determine the level of their physical involvement as their relationship enters engagement and races toward the altar. Many respond that they believe their physical involvement should become intense and intimate prior to marriage.

On one level, such logic sounds great. "The more I get to

know you, the more I get from you." If you follow this logic, then it makes sense that a couple would engage in every sexual expression with each other prior to marriage except sexual intercourse, which is clearly prohibited until after marriage.

Usually, one of the arguments for this position is the belief that if you don't get involved with each other *prior* to marriage, you won't know what to do *in* marriage. Let me assure you that sex is one area where you can pretty much follow your instincts—you won't need an instruction manual on your wedding night. Furthermore, one's wedding night is clearly an instance in which the adage "If at first you don't succeed, try, try again" is quite easily applied!

Another argument has to do with wanting to be sure you are sexually compatible. The non-Christian world uses this logic to justify living together before marriage. The statistics are clear: such experimentation before marriage leads to increased dissatisfaction after marriage. If you don't have a physical attraction for each other, by all means don't move ahead. You *should* be fighting tooth and nail to make it to the altar sexually pure. You don't need to fondle each other to know that there is chemistry there. And besides, just as with living together, fondling before marriage is no barometer of sexual compatibility in marriage.

Part of the problem with the "parallel thinking" paradigm is that it does not take into account the God-created urge to finish the sexual act once sexual stimulation begins. What is often termed an "accident" is simply the result of a couple not stopping their bodies from completing the cycle that God put in place: the cycle that starts with sexual stimulation and ends with climax and release.

The other problem with parallel thinking is found in scripture. Matthew 5:28 is pretty clear that we are not to lust after another person.[1] If "lusting" is being sexually involved with someone other than your spouse in thought or deed, then being sexually stimulated by your partner prior to marriage would seem to constitute lust.

The Biblical guidelines for sexual conduct are not on a sliding scale, as much as we would like to believe they are. What's more, instead of having *deeper* physical involvement the closer they get to marriage, many couples would be wise to *restrict* their physical involvement as they approach their wedding.

We met with an engaged couple who had decided not to kiss until they were engaged. We applauded them for their self-control and the intentional guidelines they had set. When we asked them how they were doing physically as their wedding day approached, they responded by saying that they had placed more stringent boundaries around their physical expression so that they would not have to struggle to "stay pure."

When your mother and I returned from our honeymoon, a number of friends asked me what we had done for our trip. I usually would answer, "We went 'sight seeing.'" Our friends would continue their questioning and ask where we went. I would then get a smile on my face and say, "Oh, we stayed in our cabin—there were so many sights we had never seen before!" I wish for you, too, the joy of exploration within the safety and covenant of marriage.

Many a couple has followed parallel tracks, only to end up in a train wreck. May you find incredible freedom and joy in following God's word wholeheartedly, and enjoy the blessings of such obedience.

I love you girls—
Dad

Sexual Stimulation
Is for Marriage

Dear Kari, Lisa, and Julie,

We just got word of a friend of yours who is single and pregnant. She no longer is involved with the father of the child and is facing a lot of difficult decisions as she looks to her future.

I know I have been writing a lot on the area of physical involvement, but I feel so brokenhearted when I see the results of premature sexual involvement, whether or not it leads to pregnancy, that I need to say more. As I have stated in previous letters, it is so very important to have your standards for physical involvement based on God's word and established before you are deep in the relationship.

A young man who wanted me to help hold him accountable for his physical involvement with his girlfriend asked me one day if I felt it was OK for him and his girlfriend to smell each other's armpits. He said that it was quite sexually stimulating to them both. (I've heard of many avenues to sexual stimulation, but never by smelling a partner's armpits!) I tried to keep a straight face as I carried on a conversation with this young man, explaining that the core issue is not what *part* of the body is sexually stimulating, but at what *time* in the relationship is sexual stimulation acceptable.

Some areas of involvement are sexually stimulating for virtually everyone, such as French kissing and fondling the genitals. Problems arise, however, when we arbitrarily list areas that are off bounds because they are sexually stimulating, and then argue that if some other area is not on the list, it must be OK.

For one couple, giving back rubs may be sexually stimulating, and for another, it may be holding each other closely on the couch. For other couples it may be rubbing each other's legs—or smelling each other's armpits. When we hold fast to a prescribed list, we become pharisaical and miss the heart of God in this matter. Song of Solomon says, "Do not stir up or awaken love until the appropriate time" (HCSB).[1] I believe this means we are not to excite each other sexually until we are ready to culminate the sexual act in marriage.

Someone may say, "But holding hands is sexually stimulating," or a young man might argue, "I get sexually stimulated involuntarily at times." I am not speaking of this natural physiological response. What I am speaking about is any activity that has sexual arousal as a goal.

God has designed sexual arousal to be very pleasurable. Couples easily mistake this pleasure for true intimacy and then allow themselves to continue to deeper levels of physical involvement because it feels so much like love.

I don't know what went on in your friend's relationship that eventually led to their deep physical involvement, but I would bet that at some stage they started intentionally stimulating each other sexually—and the rest, as they say, is history. In this case, a sad one.

I wouldn't write so much about this except I know there are very few people who are even considering *not* being heavily involved physically with their boyfriends and girlfriends.

I was with a seminarian recently who seemed to balk at my conservative position. My response to him was that I believe we are called on as Christians to be able to justify all our behavior by scripture. Yes, I know scripture does not specifically direct us to brush our teeth or to eat five servings of fruits and vegetables every day, but it does give us all we need to know in principle— and more specifics than we often wish to hear.

> It is so very important to have your standards for physical involvement based on God's word and established before you are deep in the relationship.

For instance, just as scripture calls us to take care of our "temples,"[2] so it calls us not to let a hint of sexual immorality be named among us.[3] As I have written before, scripture actually does say a great deal about our sexual lives. It says, for instance, that we are not to lust.[4] When we intentionally stimulate each other sexually before marriage, we lust after that which is not yet appropriate for us.

Let me end by saying that I fully realize that life is not over for your pregnant girlfriend or for others who have been sexually promiscuous. God is a God of redemption and grace and He delights in forgiving us and helping us move on to fullness of life. *But*, all the choices your girlfriend now faces are difficult at best: abortion, single parenthood, or adoption.

I can hear you saying as you read this, "*Da-ad*, it's not going to happen to us!"—and I believe you. I am sure your friend would have said the same thing. I just want to encourage you to continue to be willing to take the minority stand on physical involvement prior to marriage.

Smelling armpits? Probably not your greatest risk. May God alert you to the areas that *are* risks for you and give you the strength to honor Him in all your relationships.

Please know I write these things to you because I love you and think you all are incredibly beautiful. I so want for you to find a man who will love you enough not to enter into a sexually stimulating relationship with you... before marriage.

I love you, girls—
Dad

Your Mom Says It's
the Best Gift I Gave Her

Dear Kari, Lisa, and Julie,

Your mom told a group of teens at camp this morning that the greatest gift I had ever given her was respecting her enough not to get physically involved with her while we were dating. I don't know if that statement means I have given her very few gifts, or that *that* one was particularly meaningful to her. I trust the latter! I remember once telling her, while we were "just friends," that I had decided not to kiss a girl until the day I asked her to marry me. I asked her what she thought of that, and she said she thought it was the stupidest thing she had ever heard. (So then I said, "I wasn't serious—let's make out!"... no, I'm just kidding.) Eventually, before we started dating, she agreed to the decision not to kiss before engagement. I requested that boundary because I realized I could easily let the physical become a dominant force in our relationship since your mom was so beautiful.

We ended up dating for over a year and a half before our first kiss (on December 15, 1975, the day I asked her to marry me). During that time we became very creative in how we showed our affection for each other. In our attic, we have a chest full of poems, cards, and invitations to all sorts of crazy events. The message on one homemade posterboard card that your mom gave me was completely made of empty candy wrappers. (She knew even then that *full* candy wrappers were not a beneficial gift for me.) Her card was wonderfully creative—I don't remember all the details of its construction, but I do remember that the first candy bar wrapper was from a U-NO bar.

Many couples show their affection for each other mainly by locking lips. We have found, in our years of counseling, that while physical involvement may be a real *attractor*, it is rarely a genuine *indicator* of true love. If sex is what is keeping a relationship together, then the couple is in real trouble: sex is a very poor glue in a marriage.

At a conference where I had just finished teaching on sex not being good glue for a relationship, a girl came up to me and said she agreed with me. She went on to say that though she and her boyfriend were involved sexually, sex wasn't at all the reason they were together. She told me how wonderful he was and how fortunate she was to have this man as her boyfriend. I responded that I was glad she had found such a great guy, but asked her how she was so confident in his love apart from sex.

"Oh, he told me that sex was not that important to him. He says he just really loves me, and sex is the natural expression of his love." I told her that if he were really as wonderful as she had described, I was sure her asking him to stop having sex with her would not hurt their relationship. She became quiet, and then confessed that she actually *had* asked him to stop having sex once before—but that he had told her that if they stopped having sex, the relationship was over. So I suggested to her that if this was the case, she should let him go—and wait for another man who would honor her as God desired her to be honored by a man. She thanked me and left. I have no knowledge of what happened to her. I wish I believed that she left him and is now married to a strong believer, but I fear she was afraid of losing him and continued to sleep with him until they married—or until he found someone he "loved more."

I am so proud of the way you girls not only have made decisions for yourselves, but also are helping other girls think through their standards. The letter you shared, Kari, from the 15-year-old girl who heard your mom and me give a relationship talk, was especially moving to me. We often think "everyone" knows this stuff, but apparently that's not true. In her letter she wrote,

> *Tell your folks thanks soooo much for their banana talk. Before their talk, I had no idea what "saving sex for marriage" was, but now I know. I just thought it was "no intercourse." Now I understand that saving sex for marriage involves not getting sexually excited with anyone other than your mate.*

It was neat that she felt free to open up and be vulnerable about her relationship with her boyfriend. I was so thrilled to hear that she went home and told her boyfriend all she had learned. I want to quote from her letter again because she said it so well:

> *When I got home, the guy who I had been physically involved with called. I was excited to tell him everything I had learned at camp. I told him about the four rules of "four on the floor, hands off, clothes on, and tongue in." After I finished, all he said was, "It's too bad you changed—we had so much fun together. I guess I better go."*

Let me take a stab at rephrasing his response in words that more clearly express what I think he meant: "It's too bad you developed some respect for yourself—I had so much fun sexually with you. I guess I better go and find someone who has no convictions so I can meet my own sexual desires." What I loved the most about her letter was her response to his call and breakup. She wrote,

> *I wasn't sad at all. I didn't want him back; I had no*
> *feelings for him. It was such a relief.*

Yes!

I long for you to find men who honor and respect you as women of God. You are all godly, fun, and creative women. I wish for you men who are the same.

Love, Dad

Emotional Hooks
in Relationships

Dear Kari, Lisa, and Julie,

For some reason, as I awakened this morning I was thinking about the "hooks" that seem to hold people in less-than-healthy relationships.

I just now got off the phone with Lisa, who was telling me about her night last night as a Resident Assistant in her dorm. I phoned her at 10 am her time, and to my surprise, my call woke her up. I asked her why she was still sleeping, and she explained that she hadn't gotten to bed until 3 am—because she had had to help several drunken students get to bed. She told me about one student in particular with whom, just two nights before, she had had a conversation about his drinking in high school. He told Lisa what a bad decision that had been and how he was going to start anew at the university. Two nights later he was passed out drunk on the floor.

It reminds me of our study at camp this last summer: the children of Israel were miraculously freed from hundreds of years of slavery, only to long to return to Egypt after facing some discomfort in the desert. How prone we are to soon return to that which enslaves us in unhealthy ways!

The same hooks that tend to pull us back into unhealthy

relationships also make us more prone to get involved in unhealthy relationships in the first place. But the hooks are generally different for men and for women. The physical or sexual side of a relationship tends to be the "hook" for a man, while the emotional or relational side of the relationship tends to be the "hook" for a woman.

I'll never forget meeting with a man who had been married for 15 years. He told me how miserable he was in his marriage. He said that virtually every day, in his presence, his wife would apologize to her children that she had married such a loser for a husband or say how sad she was that her children had to have such a dad. She ridiculed him continually. I asked him if she had been so critical before they were married. "Oh, yes," he replied, "but the sex was so good I wasn't willing to give up the relationship. And besides, I figured after we got married, things would change. I was right, things did change: there was no sex after marriage, only nagging and criticism."

A Christian woman friend of ours informed us that she, at age thirty, was about to marry a non-Christian man. "I know it's wrong," she said, "but I have 'done it right' for thirty years and I'm still single. I want to be married and have a relationship with a man, so I am taking things into my own hands." And that she did—she married the non-Christian man and has been miserable ever since. She was hooked by her emotional needs, seemingly filled by this man, and was blinded to the objective truth that should have guided her in her decision.

It is interesting to note how we use the word "hooked." We will say, "he got hooked on pornography." Or, "she got hooked on romance novels." Men seldom get hooked on romance novels and women seldom get hooked on pornography. Knowing our areas of vulnerability, we need to be especially careful.

Each of you would like to be married someday. We've often talked together about setting physical boundaries in relationships, but I don't know that we have given adequate time to the area of emotional boundaries.

Often your mom and I will hear a couple say, "we couldn't help ourselves—the relationship just developed so fast!" We will then talk to them about making a firm decision to refrain from physical involvement in order to "slow down" the relationship. "But there is no way of stopping the way we *feel* for each other," many will say. We disagree; there *are* ways to slow down one's emotional involvement as well.

We know a couple (you know them, too) who are "boyfriend and girlfriend," yet are only sophomores in college, have made the decision to talk together no more than twice a week and to e-mail each other no more than three times a week. They have acknowledged that if their relationship does continue on to marriage, it will not be for a number of years yet. They are wise to "pace" the relationship.

How can you safeguard and pace your emotions?

Control the amount of time you spend together. Even if you live in the same area, you don't need to hang out alone together every evening.

Don't isolate yourselves. Spend time with other friends in groups. Don't be possessive and jealous and afraid that your boyfriend may have looked at another girl. This time in your lives—before marriage—is the very time a young man is supposed to use to make sure you are *the one*. Only insecure people try to shelter their boyfriends or girlfriends from other relationships.

Avoid talking about your "future together" or about "if we were married." For most girls, such conversations are as physical foreplay is to most men. Avoid conversations that prematurely include phrases such as "I love you," "There will never be anyone else like you," and "I'll always be there for you."

It is not helpful for a male to fantasize what sex will be like with his girlfriend. Similarly, it is not helpful for a female to fantasize what marriage will be like with her boyfriend. Fantasy is addictive because everything always turns out as you wish, but real life seldom turns out that way.

One of the most effective safeguards against premature emotional attachment is to have healthy relationships with God, with your family, and with other believers of the same and opposite sexes. You *can* pace your relationship.

I love you, girls, and I so want you each to be married to the man who will, in reality, give you that which you have always dreamed of.

Love, Dad

How Do I Know If He Has Truly Changed?

Dear Kari, Lisa, and Julie,

Have I told you how much we have loved having you all home this Christmas? These last few days have been especially fun with your college friends from camp hanging out with us. Your mom and I feel so very privileged to be included in the late night sledding expeditions, Cranium tournaments, etc.

Kari, I really appreciated the question you posed a couple days ago and have been pondering it ever since. You asked how to know when the areas in a guy's life that once seemed to you like "relationship stoppers" should be reconsidered as only "minor differences." The reason I see this as such a terrific question is because it is one that often occurs in relationships that grow cold and then reignite. A couple may break up over some issue, and then one or both start missing the "good times" they had together and begin to rationalize or minimize the problem areas that led to their break-up.

What makes us all so vulnerable to going back to a former dating relationship is that "going back" is a known quantity. It's probably a relationship that brought you some satisfaction or you wouldn't have been there in the first place. And when one is home alone every night remembering the "good times" with a former boyfriend or girlfriend, it is especially hard to resist the temptation to initiate the relationship again.

There are actually two separate questions to consider before returning to a former relationship. First, are the areas that initially seemed to be a problem in the relationship truly not a problem after all? (Perhaps they are just little, inconsequential differences?) Second, if there were truly unacceptable differences, has the person so genuinely changed that you feel you can safely resume the relationship?

Let's examine the first question: are the areas not a problem after all? When your mom and I were going together, her laugh bothered me for some reason. It sounds silly now, but at the time, I couldn't imagine living with someone who laughed like that. Obviously, either her laugh has changed, or—what is more likely—I eventually realized it was not a big deal. I love her laugh now, so I can't imagine what was wrong with me.

The second question concerns the genuineness of changed behavior. Just last night, one of you told us about a friend of yours who broke up with her boyfriend because he wasn't treating her well. You told us that after their breakup, they had not seen or talked with each other again for an extended period of time. During that time, the guy had the opportunity to date other girls and soon realized what a treasure he had had in your friend. He then sought counsel from trusted adults and asked if in fact he had been "a jerk" in the relationship. When they answered in the affirmative, he took their advice seriously and made substantial changes in his life. Your friend has told you that her relationship with him is entirely different now. Certainly she will want to let some time pass to make sure that his change is genuine and permanent, but it looks good so far.

One of you recently told us about a male friend of yours who had just quit drinking and smoking. When we asked what led to this change, you responded, "His new girlfriend didn't want him to smoke or drink." In this type of situation, you would so want to *make sure* that the reason for changed behavior is personal conviction and not simply a change to please another person. Yes, there can be times where a person will genuinely say, "Out of love for you and what you are comfortable with, I will (or will not) do something for the rest of my life." On the other hand, if this change is merely a way to "win" the guy or girl and is not a genuine change of heart, the likelihood of it being a lifelong change is slim. I remember that the hired hands on my parents' farm were told they would have to give up drinking if it made them late for work and less productive. In order to keep their jobs, they would change—for a while—but eventually, they didn't show up for work. The change was just too hard.

Your mom once met with a woman whose boyfriend would always go to church—when she did. When the girlfriend was away, however, the boyfriend always had an "excuse" for why he couldn't attend. This certainly was an indicator that his "change" in behavior would be evident only as long as he wanted to please her.

So, how do you know if the change is real? Consider how your friend talks about the activity or area of life that has changed. Does he talk about the "good ol' days" when he was involved in this activity? Does he talk about having changed because of *you* (rather than reflecting on the rightness of his decision to change)?

If the area of change had to do with leadership: have you truly observed growth in his leadership, or do you find yourself beginning to say his leadership may not be that important after all?

If the area of change is one of obedience to God's Word: do you now observe him making decisions that are not popular or that might cause him personal sacrifice—because it is the biblical thing to do?

One last thought on this actually comes from an unrelated conversation I had with Ray Johnston regarding how to know when it is time to change jobs. He believes that one should accept a new position only when one feels *called* to the new position—rather than simply running away from an old position one doesn't like. In the context of relationships, this could be restated as: you should restart a former relationship only when your desire really is to pursue a new relationship with your former friend, not because you dislike your current relationship—or lack of one.

We have a dear friend who once dated a man in our church. He treated her poorly and often pushed the physical boundaries. Disgusted by his "two-faced life," she stopped seeing him. Soon after she developed a relationship with a man who treated her with respect and honor in every way. She was quite sure marriage was on the horizon. When this man abruptly ended the relationship, she was devastated. Before long she returned to the "two-faced" man and allowed him to take advantage of her in her broken and vulnerable state.

We always make our best decisions out of a full and satisfied life rather than out of an empty and dissatisfied life.

May God continue to be the ultimate source of your wholeness, significance, and worth. May He then guide you to (or back to) the person who will be the best partner in life.

I love you—
Dad

How Do You Know the "Real Deal"?

Dear Kari, Lisa, and Julie,

How great to have you all home together before we go off to camp for the summer!

Last week, I was talking to a man about his growing relationship with a young woman he's been dating. We were discussing similarities and differences between him and his girlfriend. When we started talking about their physical involvement in past relationships, some significant differences arose. He had been very careful to avoid physical involvement with his girlfriends, while his present girlfriend had pretty much done everything except actual intercourse with her previous boyfriends.

As we talked, the man told me how good he felt about their decisions together regarding how physically involved to become at this stage of their relationship. I affirmed him for this, and then asked him how he would be able to determine whether his girlfriend's physical boundary decisions were her own. That is, were they from a genuine change in her convictions, or were they merely in response to his lead? I could see some disappointment on his face as he tried to convince me that she truly had changed. I was not implying otherwise, but simply wanted to raise the issue that whenever there is a significant change in someone's behavior, we do ourselves a favor if we carefully investigate why the change took place and seek to confirm its genuineness.

A mentoring pastor once told me a story about his daughter, Margaret. She was in seventh grade, was very cute, and was the object of many a young man's attention. For some reason she seemed drawn to boys with a bit of a wild side. As the story goes, she came home one day to tell her father that she had a new boyfriend and his name was Billy. The father happened to know that Billy had a horrible reputation at school. He often missed class (and when he did come he was always tardy), seldom did his homework, and was all around a teacher's worst nightmare. The father, very wisely, did not prohibit her from seeing Billy, but said it could only be at school in public places—and only if Billy started becoming "responsible." Margaret was a strong young lady and she actually agreed with her father that Billy would have to change if the relationship were to develop. Over the next few weeks, the teachers observed a miracle, second in their minds only to the parting of the Red Sea[1]: Billy started coming to class—every class, every day, and on time! He started doing his homework and turning it in on time. Oh, what some young men will do for love! It appeared that irresponsible, irritating, irascible Billy had been transformed into a dependable, polite, responsible "William." Unfortunately, it only *appeared* to be a transformation, for after

> Don't fall for a guy who is "smitten" with you and who will become whatever he needs to in order to have you.

four weeks of this new life, even love could not keep up the façade. The *real* Billy, deep down inside, was still the *old* Billy. In order to please Margaret he had sucked it up for a few weeks, but that was all he could muster.

I tell you this story to illustrate the point with the young man I was counseling. Was his girlfriend's desire to be in a relationship so strong, and her need so deep, that she followed the lead of whatever man she was involved with at the time? Was she afraid that if she stood up for what she truly believed that she would lose him? Was she willing to compromise her values with each of these former boyfriends just so she could maintain the relationships she so desired? *Or*, was her former behavior actually indicative of her true values, and was she now conforming to the values of my counselee in order to keep this new relationship? I asked him if he knew *when* she had come to the realization that her involvement with these other men was inappropriate? How many men prior to him had she "held her ground" with?

Obviously, I am concerned that you not fall for a guy who is "smitten" with you and who will become whatever he needs to in order to have you.

Again, time is an important ingredient in observing how genuine change is. When you talk about your standards with your date, does he truly agree—or does he simply go along because it is your standard? Does he make statements like, "That's fine for you, but don't expect everyone to take your position"? Is he defensive about his past relationships as "really not that bad"? Do you suspect that if you let down your guard, he would pursue more physical involvement than you are comfortable with?

Always look as far back as you are able in order to see patterns of behavior.

Finally, let me affirm that God is able to radically change lives, and I don't for a minute want to suggest that I doubt His power. But I do want to state that lives are genuinely changed in response to *Him* and not in response to any other person.

When Jesus told Peter to let down his nets again to catch fish and Peter then realized who Jesus was, he asked Jesus to depart from him.[2] I think I would have been inclined to ask Jesus to become my fishing partner—after all, life is better with Jesus! But, no, we do not follow Jesus primarily so life can be better; we follow Him because He is Lord. The only appropriate response when we first see Jesus is to fall down before Him because we finally see the wickedness of our sins.

If someone is *genuinely* changed, it will be because he came into contact with the living God—not just some gorgeous, athletic, talented, skilled, intelligent, disciplined, gifted person.

You can tell if your watch is genuinely waterproof only by holding it under water.

Love you, Dad

Marriage by Choice, Not Obligation

Dear Kari, Lisa, and Julie,

I spoke this morning to a group of mothers on "Growing Christian Kids." Thanks for the decisions you have made in life that give your mom and me the platform to speak about our family, not to mention countless humorous illustrations. You have also given us such joy as parents and a message of hope for parents along the way. Thanks for following Jesus even when we have, at times, disappointed you as parents.

Earlier this week, a man came in to see me. He came alone, because his wife had refused to join him. He told me that soon after they began dating, she asked him if he loved God. It seemed very important to her. He said he did, and their relationship continued. Soon after, she found herself pregnant by him and they decided to marry. Things were going well for them in the early years of marriage. They bought a house, had a child, lived near her family in a warm climate, etc. When he was transferred to a colder climate, she followed. However, she never really connected with any new friends, and she definitely did not like the weather. Eventually, they bought a small farm, and she seemed excited about their life together there. His job involved traveling during the week, and on the weekends he often worked odd jobs to earn more money, plus he volunteered at the local fire department whenever he could. She began to feel isolated, abandoned, and unloved by her husband—who seemingly had time for everything but her.

I asked the man how he thought his wife would answer this question: "I would feel more loved by my husband if…" He immediately said, "If I were more romantic, took her on dates, courted her, and spent time with her." I looked at him and said, "I bet she has never felt chosen by you. She most likely feels that you 'had' to marry her—and if it had not been for the pregnancy, she would have been just another notch on your belt."

The man replied that I was exactly right (that doesn't happen very often!), and that whenever he *does* do something for his wife, she claims he does it only because he knows he is *supposed* to. She wants him to spontaneously take initiative with her: buy her things without her asking, take her out without her suggesting it, and so on. *She wants to feel chosen, cherished, and loved.*

Many people get into sexual relationships without any idea of the lifelong ramifications. He felt he was doing the right thing—he married her. That didn't seem very romantic to her.

When a man and a woman engage sexually with each other—and especially when they become pregnant—they will sometimes marry because "it's the right thing to do." What they both struggle with (and often the woman most intensely) is the exact thing this couple were struggling with: "Would I have been chosen if we hadn't had sex? Would I have been chosen if we hadn't become pregnant?"

Last night, I was watching the news and channel surfing during the commercials (it's the only kind of surfing I have ever been successful at). I came across a show where an older man and woman were staring into each other's eyes over dinner. My attention was caught when she said, "The only way I'll marry you is if we have a prenuptial agreement." I immediately assumed she was filthy rich and he was a pauper. The opposite turned out to be true: he was the wealthy millionaire, and she the lower-income worker. She wanted the prenuptial so there would be no question in his mind *why* she was marrying him. "I want you to know that I love you for *you*—and not for your position or wealth."

As odd as this sounds, and as much as I am against prenuptials, I applauded the sentiment: "I am not marrying you because of your wealth." Likewise "I am not marrying you because we are pregnant."

The choice to spend your entire life with another person is such an important decision that it should be made without unnecessary pressures. The courtship phase of a relationship is like no other. How amazing it is to know that out of all the men or women in the world, you have been chosen by another! I remember vividly that December night in 1975 on the beach in San Diego when I proposed to your mom. First, I offered her a Certs—which should have been a big hint, since I had told her I would not kiss her until we were engaged. After I asked *the question*, she told me she would have to think about it—and after the longest 3 seconds of my life, she said "Yes."

Yes! She said "*yes*" to me—she chose *me* to be her husband for the rest of our lives. She chose *me* over any other man in the world. That's pretty neat. She chose *me*—not because she was carrying our child, not because we had been physically intimate and she felt guilty for it, and not because she was drunk and didn't know what she was doing. With sound mind and as objective a thought process as could be expected given my charm and good looks, she chose *me*—"and now you know the rest of the story."

I know that each of you have made a commitment to sexual purity, but I also realize that you are living in a culture where most people do not recognize the incredible wisdom of God when He said that a couple need to become independent from their families, make a life-long commitment to each other, and only then celebrate their relationship by becoming one within the security of this life-long commitment.

Oh, girls, do you get tired of me writing it again? God is so good, and in His love He has given us a way to live that greatly reduces the pain and increases the joy we may experience in life—by living *according to His Word.*

Thanks for your love for God and for His Word. I echo the words of 3 John, verse 4: "I have no greater joy than to hear that my children are walking in the truth."

Thanks for giving your mom and me such great joy!

Love, Dad

It's Never Too Late to Do the Right Thing

Dear Kari, Lisa, and Julie,

Today, we received the great news that George and Donna had a healthy baby boy yesterday morning. This is such great news—they had so wanted to have a child, but were unable to get pregnant. Donna believed it was because they had "lived in sin" before they were married and God was now punishing them.

I'll never forget the first time I met George and Donna. They were new to our church and wanted to get married. They signed up for an appointment with me to discuss the possibility of my officiating at the service. After making the appointment, our wedding consultant mailed them the church wedding policy on being married at Grace Chapel.

When they came in, they immediately stated that they had read the information packet and saw that the church had a policy against marrying couples that were currently living together. To their credit, they stated they were living together and wanted to know why that would disqualify them from being married at our church. I mentioned that it was not as much a church issue as it was an issue of obedience to scripture.

Before we went any further, I asked them to tell me a bit

about themselves. Donna started with her story: she had been in an abusive marriage when she was quite young, which ended in divorce. George then told his story: he had never been married before, but had been brought up in a divorced marriage situation. They explained how they had met and initially chose to move in together for "economic" reasons, but before long were sleeping together.

I asked them to describe their religious experience. He said he was from a Roman Catholic background, but that it had not been an integral part of his life in recent years. She shared that she had been brought up as a Southern Baptist. As they went on to share more, it seemed that she at one time had truly had a vital relationship with the Lord, while he, most likely, had never really committed his life to the Lord in a personal way.

We talked for a while about why the scriptures direct us not to be sexually involved with someone until we are husband and wife. We talked about trust, getting to know each other outside of the sexual relationship, obedience to what scripture taught, and so on.

I asked why they had chosen to enter into a sexual relationship. He said that after all the hurt of being raised in a divorced family, he swore he would never do that to his children, so he wanted to live with the woman to make sure they would never get divorced. I then explained to him that statistically he had increased his chances of divorce by living with Donna.

Donna, it seemed, just went along with it since George seemed to be so caring toward her, something she had not experienced in her first marriage.

I then told them that the other issue they would have to deal with was their respective spiritual positions. I explained that scripture is quite clear on the necessity of a believer marrying only another believer. I told them I really liked them and would be honored to do their wedding if they stopped being sexually active, if Donna recommitted herself to the Lord, and if George became a Christian. I suggested they move apart, become sexually abstinent, and continue to explore making a choice to follow Christ fully.

Before they left, I said, "I appreciate your honesty about sleeping together, but why did you tell me if you knew it was against the stipulations for marriage in the church?" "Well," said Donna, "I couldn't lie to you, that would be sin." In tears, she added, "I know what you're thinking: 'You won't lie to me, but you have no problem sleeping with your boyfriend.'"

They left—and I assumed I would never see them again. In our town, there were many pastors who would not hesitate to marry them.

The next week I went into the office and saw an appointment with George and Donna in the daily appointment book. I assumed they had originally signed up for two appointments and simply never called in to cancel. I was glad I would have an extra hour to get caught up on some paperwork. Therefore, I was a bit shocked when Donna and George knocked on my door to keep their appointment! I welcomed them in and asked, "How can I assist you today?" They said, "We discussed what you said and we believe you are right, so we have decided to move apart." They had been living together for over a year and shared quite a bit of furniture. Donna asked if it was okay to keep their furniture together. I assured her that scripture says nothing about "unequally yoked furniture."

To make a long story short, they moved into separate housing and kept coming to church. Eventually George committed his life to Christ and I kept my word and married them. While pictures were being taken after the service, I overheard the photographer instruct Donna to get closer to George. She looked at me and said, "I guess we can be as close as we want now!"

I tell this story to illustrate the saving grace of God. It is never too late to start doing the right thing. Both George and Donna have told many others contemplating marriage that their moving apart was the best decision they made.

They have struggled with some of the ramifications of sinful choices they made before marriage, but overall have done really well. God loves to bless those who turn to Him in obedience and turn away from that which is sinful. He does not "get even" with us for past sinful choices, but loves to lavish us with His blessings.

Baby Peter is one of the blessings of God.

I write this to you, not because I believe you will make the choices George and Donna did, but because I am fully aware that many of your friends have made and are making decisions apart from God's will. Let us never forget that God is a God of second chances. He delights when we turn from sin and turn to Him.

I love you each so much and trust you will continue to make choices that save you from pain. I also trust that you will always be messengers of hope to those who need to hear God's invitation to accept His forgiveness.

Love, Dad

Concluding Thoughts

Will He Encourage Your Passions?

Dear Kari, Lisa, and Julie,

What an incredible joy it was for me to have us all together in Trinidad this last week. I loved being with you. Thanks for all the support you gave me as I led the team. Your mom and I are so proud of each of you. To see you interact with the children, lead sessions, and converse with adults is a gift beyond words to us as Christian parents. To think that you, Julie and Lisa, chose to spend your vacation week, and you, Kari, were willing to do the extra work to take a week off from school, all to do ministry—that's pretty neat. One of my greatest regrets as you get older is that someday your mom and I will do these ministry events without any of you. So often it is *your* presence—your interaction together, with us, and in ministry to others—that actually has the most impact at these occasions.

Lisa and Kari, I'm sorry your trips back to your schools were so eventful. Kari, I am proud of you for not taking the first "no" from the airline personnel. If you had, you might still be in Miami! I know I have said this before, but I want to express again how thankful I am that you are each such strong ladies. I do wish for you to have husbands someday who will share the load so you will not always have to be the strong ones.

While we were in Trinidad, your mom and I had the opportunity to counsel a young couple who were both in full-time Christian ministry and were contemplating the next step in their relationship. I may eventually write to you about a number of topics we covered with them, but in this letter I want to focus on just one issue.

The young woman had a passion for ministry and had always wanted to go to Bible school and then be a missionary to India. The young man said that if she went to Bible school, they would have to break up, because he didn't want to "wait" two years for her while she was gone. She was upset because, as she saw it, she had two options: pursue her passions and dreams and go to school and the mission field, but let go of her relationship with this young man; or marry him, but let go of her ministry passions. When she spoke of ministry, her eyes lit up and her voice became quite animated. When she spoke of marriage, she got teary and spoke of all the dreams she would have to let go of because of her role as wife and mother.

The question that came out of the discussion was, "How do you know when it is right to marry?" This, I would say, is the 64,000 dollar question.

Each letter I have written you contains, I hope, some piece of the answer to this question. Ultimately, of course, you must each make a decision that you alone take responsibility for. You will take into account many aspects of a man's character, abilities, personality, charm, etc. But in the end, you don't use a score card and allot points to each quality. You should not walk down the aisle saying, without emotion, "Well, he *did* score an 85 out of 100. I'm sure I will learn to overlook the 15 points I can't stand!"

So, *how do you know?* We do not want to suggest in any way that we are the matchmakers—that is God's department. We do, however, have a few ideas that we shared with the couple that night that I will pass on to you.

1) *Would your regret be greater if you walked away from your dreams for marriage, or if you walked away from marriage and pursued your passions?*

I am not suggesting that getting married and pursuing your passions are mutually exclusive. For many couples, their marriage and their individual passions all coexist quite nicely. There are times, however, when the passions of two individuals are quite different and simply can not be pursued simultaneously. This was the case here. There was no question that each really enjoyed the other and that they were quite open to spending their life together. The problem was that when he spoke of marriage, she perceived it as a jail sentence that would prevent her from experiencing life and ministry as she had always dreamed. For him, joining her in her dreams and passions would have felt like imprisonment.

The question we often ask a couple is, "If you broke up tomorrow and would never see each other again, how would you feel?" If the answer from either is "It would make me sad, but I'm sure I'd find someone else," it is a pretty good indication that a breakup may not be such a bad thing. On the other hand, if the answer from each is "I can't even imagine it—I would rather be with him/her doing anything, than pursuing my dreams by myself," they should consider finding a good jeweler.

2) *If you marry and don't pursue your passions, you may always be tempted by "what if?"*

To marry because someone told you to, because you didn't want to hurt his feelings, or because it seemed the "right" thing to do, may lead to second-guessing during the rough times of marriage.

3) *If you pursue your dreams and they turn into a nightmare...*

... you still have the option to return to the relationship if the other person also desires to pursue this option. Dreams that don't work out are a bummer. Marriages that don't work out are disasters.

4) *Always remember that time is your friend.*

If God wants you together, He is able to confirm that in both your minds and hearts. Don't ever rush a relationship just so the other person won't change his or her mind.

5) *Don't get engaged so you can put someone on the "layaway" plan while you pursue your dreams.*

There is nothing wrong with a long-distance relationship while you are pursuing education or various unique experiences. However, premature engagement to ensure you will not date someone else while you are apart only speaks of great insecurity. Remember, if God has chosen you for each other, separation will make the heart grow fonder, not colder.

~

Basically, all I am saying is another version of your mom's statement: "It takes a really great husband to be better than no husband at all." Wait for the man you can't wait to marry, rather than marry because you just can't wait.

Your mom had always dreamed of being a missionary to a Spanish-speaking country. She was Spanish major and spent a summer immersing herself in the Spanish culture in Guadalajara. Then she met me, and, as they say, the rest is history. For her, there came a point when she decided she would rather spend her life with me than alone doing missionary work in a Spanish-speaking country. I am (obviously!) glad she made that decision. God in His kindness has given her many ways to use her Spanish for ministry over the course of our marriage. *But*, there was a day when she had to make a decision.

Keep walking faithfully with God and He will direct your paths—even to the altar. It's His promise.

Love, Dad

This Decision Will Affect the Rest of Your Life!

Dear Kari, Lisa, and Julie,

Last week, I received a frantic phone call from a mom whose daughter is engaged to be married in eight weeks. Her daughter met a man while on a semester abroad program and came home with more than just credit for another semester at school—she came home with a fiancé. Her mom is very concerned. The man does not have a relationship with Christ as her daughter does. The two have known each other for only three months. Furthermore, the young man has not held a job for the past three years. Finally, he managed to offend every family member present at a recent family gathering. The mom is sure he wants to hurry the wedding just so they can have sex—and they are not involved now?

When I asked about the relationship between the father and the daughter, the mom answered that it was distant. In fact, she told me that the father believes that marrying this man will teach his daughter some valuable lessons in life. My heart ached for this family as I imagined the sorrow ahead for them all. A couple years ago, I started off this series of letters by stating that the decision of whom to marry will be the second most important decision of your life. I feel more passionately about this today than ever. Let me use this family's situation to illustrate one more time the critical nature of the decision.

Very likely, this young girl was not close to her father. He was probably too busy working and involved in his own interests to give her the attention, acceptance, affection, and love she needed. But now, she desperately wants somebody to show her attention and give her the acceptance and affection she's longed for. Enter Don Juan. He is available—since he has no job. He is affectionate —duh. He accepts her just as she is—for now. And he says he loves her—after only two days together!

The dad is an idiot. Any man who is willing to let his daughter marry the wrong man to "learn a lesson" needs more than a lesson himself. I don't know the full history of the mother and father, but I do know that she is a person of faith and he is not. How difficult to give good advice to your daughter when the two of you come from such different perspectives!

What will I advise this young woman if she comes to see us? This:

- Know the man you are about to marry. Go slow, get to know his family, and spend at least a year in relationship before making any decisions.
- Make sure he is a vital Christian. If you are not sure, most likely he isn't! Make sure that he will take initiative and lead the family in the ways of God in worship, morals and lifestyle.
- Don't get involved sexually with each other. Physical involvement has a way of clouding one's vision. Make sure he honors you in this way.
- Make sure he is a provider—that is, he has held and currently does hold a responsible job, and has a plan for his future.
- Make sure he is a man you respect, since you are called to submit to him.

- Make sure that those who know you well also approve of the relationship.
- Imagine him as a father. Will he be an unselfish servant? Will he be involved with the children? Will he be committed to you and the family above all other interests?

~

Thanks for living lives that have not necessitated too many "frantic calls" to advisors.

May God continue to lead you and may you find incredible joy as you walk with Him.

Love, Dad

Then Who Will Ever Get Married, Dad?

Dear Kari, Lisa, and Julie,

As your mom and I fly home after our time together at Thanksgiving, I am filled with gratefulness to God for giving you to us. We rejoice that after 23, 20, and 18 years, you still like to hang out with us.

While we talked together this last weekend, one of you commented, "No one will ever make it through Dad's grid," or words to that effect. It sounded a bit like the disciple's statement "It is better not to marry," made when Jesus was talking to them about God's design for marriage in Matthew, chapter 19.[1]

I will admit I have raised the bar quite high, because I so want the best for each of you. I'll admit that there is likely no one who will meet *every* criterion laid out in these letters. In my mind and from my experience, however, there are certainly levels of importance as you consider the topics covered in the letters.

This morning Caleb took us to the airport. We asked him how his sister Sally and her serious boyfriend Steve were doing. He said, "Sally loves the Lord and is committed to Him first, and the same is true for Steve, so I am sure they will make a good decision regarding their relationship."

I would put as "non-negotiable" those areas that have to do

with *convictions*. Is your suitor a strong and growing Christian? Is he committed to God's word? Is he obedient to what he understands is God's call on his life? Does he honor God and others above himself? If you have a man who has these areas in line, you are off to a great start.

Next, are areas of *character*. Is he a servant? Is he a man of integrity? Is his use of language honoring to God? Is he a man who will cherish you? These are all important. We are all growing in the areas of character. However, you want to make sure the areas not yet developed are few.

The next category is what I have called "*considerations*." Considerations have to do with common interests and similar areas of enjoyment. They undoubtedly add much camaraderie to a marriage, but are less critical to its success. You may be an outdoors person, while your mate is not. This certainly does not mean you cannot be happily married, but it will affect the things you enjoy doing together. In this area of considerations, "all the stars don't need to line up," but there should be at least enough to give some "light" to the relationship.

Another whole area is that of *chemistry*. For many couples this is the number-one determiner for the relationship. Your mom and I were at a conference, standing in line for a meal, when we struck up a conversation with a couple next to us. When we asked them about how they met, the woman said, "The first time I met my husband was at a party. He was drunk. He looked at me, told me he was going to marry me, and gave me a kiss. Well, when he kissed me, I knew he was the one! Six weeks later, we were married." I asked them not to talk to any of you! There was chemistry on that night, all right, but the man did not have much else going for him. Now she is supporting him financially, and neither he nor his wife are particularly happy about it.

How important is chemistry? *Very important!* Marriage without chemistry is like a hamburger without the patty, a car without gas, a fourth of July without fireworks—et cetera! But, as I have said before, because chemistry is so powerful, it is critical that it not be the driving force in the relationship. On the other hand, to move ahead without it is to risk a certain lack of enjoyment in the relationship. Ideally, chemistry should be something that grows in response to a person after a good amount of time has passed in your relationship. People with whom we seem to have an immediate chemistry often lose their fizzle with time. Genuine chemistry is a response that grows with another person as we spend more and more time together in a non-physical relationship. "Visa: don't leave home without it." Chemistry: don't walk down the aisle without it.

I know your mom would never have chosen me to marry if I had to meet the criteria in all the letters I have written. I am thankful that in her mind I had solid convictions, a fair amount of character, a good number of common interests, and enough chemistry to cause fireworks.

I wish the same and more for each of you.

Love, Dad

P. S. I am humbled that you each have said at some time, "Dad, I will never meet a man like you." I deeply appreciate your love, respect, and appreciation for me, but I do want to express two thoughts.

First, I am really not as wonderful as you think I am.

Second, to whatever extent you see me as wonderful today and as a measuring stick for your husband, remember, I am 30 years older than the men you are dating. I hope you do see characteristics in your spouse that I have modeled, but don't expect them to have matured to the level of a 55-year-old. What I mean is, look for developing maturity, not instant maturity.

Finishing Together

Dear Kari, Lisa, and Julie,

I am sitting in the Sacramento airport getting ready to return to Boston. My emotions are all over the place. I hate leaving you without all the "loose ends" tied up. I wish you were completely settled in your new house, Kari, and that I were there to get your furniture and finish the car "stuff." Julie, I wish I could get you settled as you start your freshman year in college. Lisa, I wish I were hanging with you for a few more days and could meet more of your friends and colleagues. I am so glad your mom is with you all, but I deeply miss being with you.

This past week has been incredible—being in Yosemite together and climbing Half Dome as a family. Thanks so much for your patience with me and my lack of physical conditioning. It meant a lot to me for you all to insist on finishing as a family, even when you could have sprinted ahead so many times.

Maybe that is why this departure seems so much more emotional: the phrase "finishing as a family" stays in my mind. Not that our family is over—however, in some ways, your childhood in the family *is* over. Each of you will go off the "exemption" box on our tax returns. Kari and Lisa will have their own cars and insurance, and Julie will establish California residency.

Looking back on these years together, I see some similarities to our hike up Half Dome. As we climbed, I thought, "I wish I had taken more time to get conditioned," "I wish I hadn't eaten so many Snickers bars," and so on. At the same time, I was so thankful to God that He had given me the strength to reach the top of the mountain with all of you.

As I look back on my life as a dad, I also see many places where I wish I had done it better or done it differently, and yet I am filled with gratitude that God has, in His goodness, met us as a family and allowed us to enjoy such a close relationship. I am thankful beyond words that each of you has chosen to follow the Lord, and that each of you has a vital relationship with Him.

Remember the brown bear and her cub that we saw as we left Yosemite? How will we ever forget that?! The mother bear was trying to coax her cub across the raging river, but the cub was afraid and wouldn't cross. Remember how many times the mother bear came back to her cub and showed it how to cross? I wondered why the mother didn't simply let the baby get on her back and carry her. That would have accomplished the crossing of the river, but not getting confidence to cross other rivers alone. That is a bit how I am feeling now. I wish I could put you each on my back and carry you over the rushing rivers of life. And yet, even as I type, with tears in my eyes, I know that this is the time of life where each of you need to cross the river on your own. Your mom and I have

> Any couple can start out laughing together, but fewer stay together when the hiking gets tough.

tried to show you how to cross, but now is the time for you to cross it without us. What gives me such great comfort is to know that you really never cross alone, since you each have made the choice to cross every river of life with Jesus leading you... but I still would love to help. I also know that our days of giving advice and instruction are not over—just different.

With all that said, what I really want you to know today is how incredibly proud I am of each of you. All three of you are more mature and gifted than I was at your ages. Your devotion to and relationship with the Lord is deeper than mine was at your age. And still it is hard not being with you all the time.

Part of the preparation for marriage is the "leaving" that children are called to do before "cleaving" to their spouses. So as sad as this time is in some respects, it is also very gratifying to know that you are "in queue" for making the second most important decision of life.

At your age you are able to set patterns that will allow you to live life fully with few regrets. I so long for you not only to do this for yourselves but also to eventually marry someone who has set healthy patterns for his life.

Remember the hike to Half Dome? One of my regrets was that I wasn't in better shape. Getting in shape, however, was not something I forgot to do the month before the hike—it was a pattern I never established.

I lost a lot of weight before your mom and I were married so I would look good for our wedding and honeymoon. But self-control in regards to food was not a pattern I had established earlier in life. Always be leery of those who lose weight or make any drastic changes just before the wedding—they are seldom long-lived changes. Be leery of anyone who is overweight and loses just to hike with you or starts becoming "spiritually conditioned" because of you. Make sure that habits are *truly* habits in your future spouse's life. Your mom is a great example of this. She is still able to wear the same size clothes she wore when we were married 27 years ago. (In fact, I think she still wears some of the *same* clothes she had when we were married!) She is an example of a woman who has set great patterns that have served her well.

The hike up Half Dome was a piece of cake for you, and much easier for your mom than for me, because all your habits of conditioning have been constant. Maintain *all* your habits of physical *and* spiritual conditioning—and you will *never regret it.*

Thanks for being willing to finish the hike together. I remember how we were all joking and laughing as we started the 18-mile hike. When we returned ten hours later, I could barely walk or talk—yet we did it together. That is what I want for you: any couple can start out laughing together, but fewer stay together when the hiking gets tough or when one member of the family hinders the others from reaching their individual goals.

May God give you men who hike with you until the end.

Love, Dad

Epilogue

It has been over five years since I started writing these letters. Much has changed in our lives, and yet much remains the same.

Kari is 26, single, yet in a serious relationship with a wonderful man. She is on staff at Bayside Covenant Church in the Sacramento area. She works with high school students and is pursuing her masters in Marriage and Family Therapy.

Lisa is 23 and single. She graduated from University of the Pacific with a bachelor's degree in sports medicine and is presently an athletic trainer for Mission Prepatory High School in San Luis Obispo. In addition, she substitutes at Mission as well.

Julie is 21 and entering her senior year at Cal Poly San Luis Obispo. She is a child development major and plans to be a pediatric occupational therapist. She is the captain of her national championship women's lacrosse team. Julie and Lisa live together and are involved at Grace Church in San Luis Obispo.

Virginia continues to be a model of Christian womanhood to our girls, an incredibly gifted counselor, speaker, and care giver to so many.

This past year we celebrated our 30th wedding anniversary, received our Doctor of Ministry degrees in Marriage and Family Therapy from Gordon-Conwell Theological Seminary, and traveled a great deal, speaking at marriage and family conferences.

All of our girls love the Lord, each other, and us. We are of all people most blessed.

Notes

Letter 4, A Man Whole Without You

1. In answer to a question from the Pharisees about divorce, Jesus says, *"Haven't you read," he replied, "that at the beginning the Creator 'made them male and female,' and said, 'For this reason a man will leave his father and mother and be united to his wife, and the two will become one flesh'? So they are no longer two, but one. Therefore what God has joined together, let man not separate."* (Matthew 19:4–6)

2. In a letter to the church at Colosse in Asia Minor, the apostle Paul writes, *"For in Christ all the fullness of the Deity lives in bodily form, and you have been given fullness in Christ, who is the head over every power and authority".* (Colossians 2:9–10)

3. Crabb, Larry. (1982). *The Marriage Builder.* Grand Rapids, MI: Zondervan.

4. In answer to a question from the Pharisees about divorce, Jesus says, *"Moses permitted you to divorce your wives because your hearts were hard. But it was not this way from the beginning. I tell you that anyone who divorces his wife, except for marital unfaithfulness, and marries another woman commits adultery."* (Matthew 19:8–9)

Letter 5, Do You Share a Love for God?

1. In a letter to the church at Corinth in Greece, the apostle Paul writes, *"Do not be yoked together with unbelievers. For what do righteousness and wickedness have in common? Or what fellowship can light have with darkness?"* (2 Corinthians 6:14)

2. Little, Paul E. (1970). *God's Will for Me and World Evangelism* (Urbana 70) Retrieved July 1, 2006, from InterVarsity's Urbana Convention site. http://www.urbana.org/_articles.cfm?RecordId=190

3. Read about King Solomon's love for many foreign women and how that affected his devotion to God in the Old Testament book of 1 Kings, chapter 11.

Letter 7, Does He Love God's Word?

1. *"The good man brings good things out of the good stored up in his heart, and the evil man brings evil things out of the evil stored up in his heart. For out of the overflow of his heart his mouth speaks."* (Luke 6:45)

2. Read the story of Jesus washing his disciples' feet in the New Testament book of John, chapter 13. He did this to demonstrate that his disciples should also serve one another, since no servant is greater than his master. Afterwards he said, *"Now that you know these things, you will be blessed if you do them."* (John 13:17)

Letter 8, Is He Glad to Go to the House of the Lord?

1. *Let us not give up meeting together, as some are in the habit of doing, but let us encourage one another—and all the more as you see the Day approaching.* (Hebrews 10:25)
2. *I rejoiced with those who said to me, "Let us go to the house of the Lord."* (Psalm 122:1)
3. Read Jesus' parable of the sower in the New Testament book of Matthew, chapter 13, verses 18 through 23.
4. Jesus speaks about how to recognize people by their "fruit" in Matthew 7:16–20.

Letter 11, He's Got to Leave Before He Can Cleave

1. *For this reason a man will leave his father and mother and be united to his wife, and they will become one flesh.* (Genesis 2:24)
2. *Children, obey your parents in the Lord, for this is right.* (Ephesians 6:1)
3. *Honor your father and your mother, so that you may live long in the land the Lord your God is giving you.* (Exodus 20:12)

Letter 13, Is He a Leader?

1. Crabb, Larry. (1998). *The Silence of Adam*, Grand Rapids, MI. Zondervan.
2. *Therefore, just as sin entered the world through one man, and death through sin, and in this way death came to all men, because all sinned—for before the law was given, sin was in the world. But sin is not taken into account when there is no law. Nevertheless, death reigned from the time of Adam to the time of Moses, even over those who did not sin by breaking a command, as did Adam, who was a pattern of the one to come.* (Romans 5:12–14)
3. Bly, Robert. (2004). *Iron John.* New York, NY: Da Capo Press.

Letter 14, Is He a True Servant?

1. *Husbands, love your wives, just as Christ loved the church and gave himself up for her to make her holy, cleansing her by the washing with water through the word, and to present her to himself as a radiant church, without stain or wrinkle or any other blemish, but holy and blameless. In this same way, husbands ought to love their wives as their own bodies. He who loves his wife loves himself.* (Ephesians 5:25–28)

2. *Do nothing out of selfish ambition or vain conceit, but in humility consider others better than yourselves. Each of you should look not only to your own interests, but also to the interests of others.* (Philippians 2:3–4)

3. Ortberg, John. (2002). *The Life You've Always Wanted* (p. 106). Grand Rapids, MI: Zondervan.

Letter 15, A Selfish Mate Is Worse Than No Mate at All

1. *"Haven't you read,"* he replied, *"that at the beginning the Creator 'made them male and female,' and said, 'For this reason a man will leave his father and mother and be united to his wife, and the two will become one flesh'? So they are no longer two, but one. Therefore what God has joined together, let man not separate."* (Matthew 19:4–6)

Letter 17, What's His Self-Control Quotient?

1. Chambers, Oswald. (1995). *My Utmost For His Highest.* Grand Rapids, MI: Discovery House Publishers.

2. "The Music Machine," an audio CD with songs for children about the fruits of the Spirit, published by Bridgestone Management (January 18, 2002), is available from Amazon.com.

Letter 19, Don't Marry a "Crude" Dude

1. Scripture speaks against coarse joking in Ephesians 5:4—
   Nor should there be obscenity, foolish talk or coarse joking, which are out of place, but rather thanksgiving.

2. *The good man brings good things out of the good stored up in his heart, and the evil man brings evil things out of the evil stored up in his heart. For out of the overflow of his heart his mouth speaks.* (Luke 6:45)

Letter 20, One... (No Longer Two)

1. In speaking about marriage, Jesus says, *"... a man will leave his father and mother and be united to his wife, and the two will become one flesh'... So they are no longer two, but one."* (Matthew 19:5–6)

Letter 21, Does He Have an "Entitlement" Attitude?

1. *Your attitude should be the same as that of Christ Jesus: Who, being in very nature God, did not consider equality with God something to be grasped, but made himself nothing, taking the very nature of a servant, being made in human likeness. And being found in appearance as a man, he humbled himself and became obedient to death— even death on a cross!* (Philippians 2:5–8)

Letter 23, I Hope He Knows How to Have Fun

1. Sister Maria and the von Trapp family were featured in the film *The Sound of Music* (1985), directed by Robert Wise.
2. In speaking to the people about why he has come, Jesus said, *"I have come that they may have life, and have it to the full."* (John 10:10)

Letter 26, How Important Are Common Interests?

1. In speaking about marriage, Jesus says, *"... a man will leave his father and mother and be united to his wife, and the two will become one flesh'... So they are no longer two, but one."* (Matthew 19:5–6)

Letter 27, Who Are Your Counselors?

1. *Plans fail for lack of counsel, but with many advisers they succeed.* (Proverbs 15:22)
2. For the entire story of Job, read the Old Testament book of Job. The story begins when Satan comes to present himself to God after spending time "roaming through the earth and going back and forth in it." *Then the Lord said to Satan, "Have you considered my servant Job? There is no one on earth like him; he is blameless and upright, a man who fears God and shuns evil.* (Job 1:7–8)
3. *What God has joined together, let man not separate.* (Matthew 19:6)

Letter 31, Male/Female Differences and Sexuality

1. *The Lord God said, "It is not good for the man to be alone. I will make a helper suitable for him."* (Genesis 2:18)

2. *The Lord is with me; I will not be afraid. What can man do to me? The Lord is with me; he is my helper. I will look in triumph on my enemies.* (Psalm 118:6–7) For more examples of Old Testament references to God as a helper, see also: Genesis 49:25, Psalm 10:14, Psalm 30:10, and Psalm 54:4.

Letter 32, You Asked about Modesty

1. *Your beauty should not come from outward adornment, such as braided hair and the wearing of gold jewelry and fine clothes. Instead, it should be that of your inner self, the unfading beauty of a gentle and quiet spirit, which is of great worth in God's sight.* (1 Peter 3:3–4)

Letter 33, Only Big Lures Catch Prize "Fish"

1. *Your beauty should not come from outward adornment, such as braided hair and the wearing of gold jewelry and fine clothes. Instead, it should be that of your inner self, the unfading beauty of a gentle and quiet spirit, which is of great worth in God's sight.* (1 Peter 3:3–4)

Letter 36, What Does God Think about Sex?

1. *Flee from sexual immorality. All other sins a man commits are outside his body, but he who sins sexually sins against his own body. Do you not know that your body is a temple of the Holy Spirit, who is in you, whom you have received from God? You are not your own; you were bought at a price. Therefore honor God with your body.* (1 Corinthians 6:18–20)

Letter 37, Don't Awaken Love Until Its Time

1. See Song of Solomon 2:7, 3:5, and 8:4. Each verse reads: *"Do not stir up or awaken love until the appropriate time."* (HCSB)

Letter 38, What Constitutes Sexual Purity?

1. Stenzel, Pam. *Sex Has a Price Tag.* (2000). This excellent DVD is available at www.pamstenzel.com.
2. The Pharisees often questioned Jesus, trying to trick him or test him. For examples, see: Matthew 19:3, Matthew 22:14–16, Mark 8:11, Mark 10:12, and Luke 11:53.

Letter 39, Four Scriptural Guidelines for Physical Involvement

1. For examples of how the Pharisees ignored the "spirit of the law," read Jesus' words to them in the New Testament book of Matthew, chapter 23.

2. *For this reason a man will leave his father and mother and be united to his wife, and the two will become one flesh.* (Matthew 19:5)

3. *It [love] is not rude, it is not self-seeking, it is not easily angered, it keeps no record of wrongs.* (1 Corinthians 13:5)

4. *Treat younger men as brothers, older women as mothers, and younger women as sisters, with absolute purity.* (1 Timothy 5:2)

5. *It is God's will that you should be sanctified: that you should avoid sexual immorality; that each of you should learn to control his own body in a way that is holy and honorable, not in passionate lust like the heathen, who do not know God; and that in this matter no one should wrong his brother or take advantage of him. The Lord will punish men for all such sins, as we have already told you and warned you. For God did not call us to be impure, but to live a holy life. Therefore, he who rejects this instruction does not reject man but God, who gives you his Holy Spirit.* (1 Thessalonians 4:3–8)

Letter 40, Four Practical Guidelines for Physical Involvement

1. Castleman, R. (1996). *True Love in a World of False Hope.* Downers Grove, IL: InterVarsity Press.

Letter 41, The Fallacy of Parallel Physical Involvement

1. *But I tell you that anyone who looks at a woman lustfully has already committed adultery with her in his heart.* (Matthew 5:28)

Letter 42, Sexual Stimulation Is for Marriage

1. See Song of Solomon 2:7, 3:5, and 8:4. Each verse reads: *"Do not stir up or awaken love until the appropriate time."* (HCSB)

2. *Do you not know that your body is a temple of the Holy Spirit, who is in you, whom you have received from God? You are not your own; you were bought at a price. Therefore honor God with your body.* (1 Corinthians 6:19–20)

3. *But among you there must not be even a hint of sexual immorality, or of any kind of impurity, or of greed, because these are improper for God's holy people.* (Ephesians 5:3)

4. *Put to death, therefore, whatever belongs to your earthly nature: sexual immorality, impurity, lust, evil desires and greed, which is idolatry.* (Colossians 3:5)

Letter 46, How Do You Know the "Real Deal"?

1. Read the story of how God brought His people out of slavery in the Old Testament book of Exodus. The miraculous escape across the Red Sea is told in Exodus, chapter 14.
2. Read the story of the miraculous catch of fish in the New Testament book of Luke, chapter 5.

Letter 51, Then Who Will Ever Get Married, Dad?

1. *Jesus replied, "Moses permitted you to divorce your wives because your hearts were hard. But it was not this way from the beginning. I tell you that anyone who divorces his wife, except for marital unfaithfulness, and marries another woman commits adultery." The disciples said to him, "If this is the situation between a husband and wife, it is better not to marry."* (Matthew 19:8–10)

Acknowledgments

This book truly did begin as a series of personal letters to Kari, Lisa, and Julie. Without them this book would have no personal audience and would never have been written. They have brought and continue to bring immense joy to my life. One of my life goals is to become what my daughters believe me to be. They have taught me much and have loved me way more than I deserve. 3 John, verse 4, states, "I have no greater joy than to know that my children are walking in the truth." Thank you, girls, for giving me so much joy.

Secondly, I will forever be thankful for the parents God gave me. They modeled God's love and care for me and modeled what it is to have a God-honoring marriage. I wish they were here to see what great choices their grandchildren are making in mates and relationships.

Thirdly, I want to thank the board of Home Improvement Ministries who have made it possible for Virginia and me to minister to singles, marrieds, and families. Special thanks to Doug and Julie Macrae, who originally said to me, "Why don't you start a ministry that encourages marriages and families?"

Fourthly, I deeply appreciate the expertise of Michael Benes of FORGE worldwide, who came alongside, understood the heart of this book, and designed the cover in two days.

Fifthly, I can not express fully enough my gratitude to Barbara and Guy Steele, who have read each page of this manuscript, edited it, and made it become a book. Barbara and Guy, your ability and creativity continue to amaze me. Thank you for who you are and all you do. May God restore the many hours of sleep you have sacrificed and give you great joy as you see people benefit by this book.

Sixthly, this book may have my name on it as the author, but it truly reflects the partnership of Virginia, my wife of 30 years. Thank you, Virginia, for all the ways you have encouraged me in this project. More importantly, I want to thank you for being the best mother to our girls I could imagine. You are fun, you are insightful, you are kind, and your love for God overflows to all those you come in contact with. They say the apple doesn't fall far from the tree. Thanks so much for being such a wonderful tree for our girls. I love you more today than yesterday, but not as much as tomorrow.

Lastly, I am fully aware that any good that comes from this book will be the work of the Holy Spirit. I am incredibly humbled to have the privilege and opportunity to share what I believe is God's truth. This book is about the second most important decision in life—marriage. I am so thankful that years ago I made the most important decision and asked Christ to become my Lord and Savior. May He receive the Glory for any good that comes from this book.

About the Author

Paul Friesen has been married for 30 years to his wife, Virginia, and they are the parents of three girls, ages 21–26. Paul and Virginia are the founders of Home Improvement Ministries (H.I.M.), a non-profit organization dedicated to equipping individuals and churches to better encourage marriages and families in living out God's design for healthy relationships.

Paul writes, teaches, and counsels. He and Virginia regularly speak together at marriage, men's, and women's conferences across the country, as well as at family and parenting seminars. They have an ongoing ministry with several professional athletic teams, a teaching partnership with Gordon-Conwell Theological Seminary and the Ockenga Institute, and direct family camps each summer with InterVarsity Christian Fellowship at Campus by the Sea on Catalina Island.

Paul and Virginia are (along with four others) co-authors of the book *Restoring the Fallen*, published by InterVarsity Press.

Paul has a Doctorate in Marriage and Family Therapy and a Master's degree in Family Ministry, both from Gordon-Conwell Theological Seminary. Before founding Home Improvement Ministries in 2003, he was on staff at Grace Chapel in Lexington, Massachusetts, where he served for nine years as the Director of Men's and Family Ministries.

Paul and Virginia's greatest joy in life is knowing that their children are "walking in the truth."